Mean Tears

In the Blue

Mean Tears

In the Blue

Two plays by
Peter Gill

Oberon Books
Birmingham · England

First published in 1987 by Oberon Books Limited
Mill Street, Aston, Birmingham B6 4BS, England. Telephone 021-359 2088.

James Hogan *Publishing Director*
Andrew Purcell CA *Managing Director*
Robert Weaver MIOP *Production Director*

Produced and printed in England by Kynoch Dataset Limited, Birmingham.
Cover painting by Michael Garady.
Front cover typography by Nick Xypnitos.
Text typeset in 'Garamond'.

ISBN 1 870259 05 X

Mean Tears was first performed on 22 July 1987 in the Cottesloe auditorium of the National Theatre, London, with the following cast:

Julian	Bill Nighy
Stephen	Karl Johnson
Paul	Garry Cooper
Celia	Hilary Dawson
Nell	Emma Piper

Directed by Peter Gill

Designed by Alison Chitty · Lighting designed by Stephen Wentworth

In the Blue was first performed on 18 March 1985 at a Studio Night in the Cottesloe auditorium of the National Theatre and subsequently was included as part of the National Theatre Studio's Festival of New Plays at the Cottesloe in November 1985, with the following cast:

Stewart	Ewan Stewart
Michael	Michael Maloney

Directed by Peter Gill

Designed by Alison Chitty · Lighting designed by Laurence Clayton

Mean Tears

Characters

Julian
Stephen
Paul
Celia
Nell

An indication of Stephen's room able to include other locations as indicated.

Scene divisions are not intended to stem the flow of action.

One

I

[JULIAN *and* STEPHEN]
[JULIAN *reading and smoking.* STEPHEN *working at some papers.*]

Julian   Listen.
              [STEPHEN *opens a letter with a knife*]

Stephen   Go on.

Julian   I never was attached to that great sect,
              Whose doctrine is, that each one should select
              Out of the crowd a mistress or a friend,
              And all the rest, though fair and wise, command
              To cold oblivion, though it is in the code
              Of modern morals, and the beaten road
              Which those poor slaves with weary footsteps tread,
              Who travel to their home among the dead
              By the broad highway of the world, and so
              With one chained friend, perhaps a jealous foe,
              The dreariest and the longest journey go.

              Isn't that great?
              [*Pause*]
              What would you say about me behind my back?

Stephen   I wouldn't say anything behind your back.

Julian   You wouldn't?

Stephen   No, I wouldn't. Anything I'd say I'd say to your face.

Julian   Oh yeah? Look at the bags under my eyes. Like what would
              you say? Is this shirt OK?

Stephen   Yeah.

Julian   It's not.

Stephen   It is.

Julian   But what would you say behind my back?

Stephen   Stop it.

Julian   My hair . . .

Stephen	I'd say.
Julian	What would you say?
Stephen	I'd say. He's got nothing and he is everything.
Julian	Fuck off, Stephen.
Stephen	What?
Julian	Fuck off.
Stephen	What?
Julian	Just fuck off. [*Pause*] I wish I could change.
Stephen	Why should you change? You're alright as you are.
Julian	But I want to change so how can you think I'm alright as I am? I should change.
Stephen	I don't want you to change.
Julian	You do.
Stephen	No fuck it. Give yourself . . .
Julian	You wish me to change.
Stephen	No.
Julian	And I should change. [*Pause*] I shall end up an old man in a hotel room.
Stephen	For fuck's sake you're young, young. Be young. or you'll <u>always</u> just be young. [*Pause*]
Julian	Stephen, why do you bother with me?
Stephen	Julian.
Julian	No, why?
Stephen	You're my representative in the world of ball games. [*Pause*]
Julian	Stephen. Are you making fun of me? Just tell me.
Stephen	No.
Julian	Are you laughing at me?

Stephen	No.
Julian	Really?
Stephen	Look. You know I'm not. Why should I be?
Julian	I just thought you might be.
Stephen	Well, I'm not. [*Pause*]
Julian	Stephen, I'm fond of you, you know. You're . . .
Stephen	Last of the good guys me.
Julian	It's just, can't you . . . ? No, forget it.
Stephen	What?
Julian	It's alright. Do you want a cup of tea?
Stephen	Oh. Christ. Julian! [*Pause*]
Julian	I'm a horrible person. Do you think I've got glandular fever?
Stephen	Yes. No. [*Pause*]
Julian	Fuck it. No cigarettes.
Stephen	You're a terrible boy, you are.
Julian	Am I? I'm not. Am I?
Stephen	You're terrible! Here. [*He gives* JULIAN *two cigarettes*]
Julian	Two? Where'd you get them? You're great.
Stephen	You're a bloody terrible boy.
Julian	You really think I am, don't you? [*Long pause*] Stephen, do you think I shall ever get married?
Stephen	Of course you will.
Julian	I don't think I shall ever get married. I shall end up an old man in a hotel room. [*Pause*]
Stephen	Did you phone home?
Julian	No. Yes.

Stephen	What did you say?
Julian	I said I was sorry.
Stephen	What about?
Julian	There was a row.
Stephen	What about? When?
Julian	Oh. Nothing, everything, the usual. Him. And them sending us away to school.
Stephen	Yes, we're all victims of the class struggle.
Julian	We fucking are.
Stephen	Are we?
Julian	Were you sent away to school?
Stephen	No.
Julian	At five? Half way across the world?
Stephen	No.
Julian	No.
Stephen	That I _was_ spared.
Julian	Oh fuck off, you.
Stephen	I _mean_ it. Come on. [*Pause*]
Julian	Stephen.
Stephen	What?
Julian	It's . . . nothing.
Stephen	What?
Julian	Was it my fault?
Stephen	How could it be your fault? It happened to you.
Julian	I thought it was my fault. I thought he'd blame me. Dad. Not locking my front door.
Stephen	But you locked the front door.
Julian	I know. That's what started the row. I threw the table over. I'm fucking glad. Was it my fault?
Stephen	How could it be your fault? It was you it happened to.

Julian	I'm sorry.
Stephen	Don't be sorry about it. There was a burglary. You were burgled. <u>You</u>. <u>You</u> were.
Julian	Do you mind? Are you angry?
Stephen	I'm not.
Julian	You are.
Stephen	Why should I be angry?
Julian	It's the insurance.
Stephen	Are you insured?
Julian	Yes.
Stephen	I'm not.
Julian	My father insured me. I fucking hate him.
Stephen	Come on, Julian.
Julian	He gave me a briefcase with a combination lock for Christmas.
Stephen	You're such a snob.
Julian	Am I? I'm not. Am I?
Stephen	Which of those alternative comedians were at university with you, Julian?
Julian	None of them. I've told you those kind of people hated me.
Stephen	Oh aye?
Julian	They did.
Stephen	Yes.
Julian	They did, Stephen. You're such a bastard. Am I a snob?
Stephen	Didn't you bonk or knob any of those girls who tell jokes about how they got thrush?
Julian	Stephen. [*Laughs*]
Stephen	No, of course most of them went to Manchester, didn't they, or Sussex, or Bangor. The thing about your mob when they do comedy is they make you realise how funny Jimmy Tarbuck is.
Julian	Well, I don't know of any Welsh humour of any sort.

Stephen	No, and there are no fucking folk songs in the Welsh coalfields either.
Julian	Yeah, and according to some sources there's no fucking coal either.
Stephen	Ohowoho. You're the only uneconomic pit round here. Were you up with Manfred M ..? No, before your time. Julian. Did you go to school with Mike D'Abo? No, no, no, no, no, no.
Julian	You're so intolerant.
Stephen	I don't know. I was very understanding when you said you liked Don't Look Now . [*Pause*]
Julian	Stephen. Do you like the Velvet Underground?
Stephen	Some of the Velvet Underground.
Julian	So you know that song I'm Waiting For The Man?
Stephen	I know that song I'm Waiting For The Man.
Julian	That's a song about heroin.
Stephen	Is it? [JULIAN *sings 'I'm Waiting For The Man'*]
Julian	I'm waiting for the man Twenty-six dollars in my hand Up to Lexington 125 This trick is dirty, more dead than alive.
Stephen	Hey you.
Julian	What? Alright. So I do heroin now and again. I can handle it. I just got a touch of flu today. That's all.
Stephen	Listen Lord Althorp. I mean it.
Julian	Would you?
Stephen	Yes.
Julian	Don't be stupid.
Stephen	[*Sings: 'I'm Waiting For The Man', laughing*]
Julian	No. You sound like Dylan. Do you like Dylan?
Stephen	Bob, yes. [*pause*] Don't roll another joint.

Julian	One more. Can I? Can I? Can I?

Stephen What do you mean can you? You've already rolled one.
[*Pause*]
What are you doing? What? You're going to veg out in front of
the telly and watch one of your Bilko tapes? As long as it's not
Hancock.

Julian 'I'd be walking round with an empty arm'.

Stephen God, please, no anything. Bruce Springsteen.
[JULIAN *begins to sing: 'Born in the* USA'. *Another agonised noise
from* STEPHEN]

Julian Don't you even like Bowie?

Stephen He's about as lasting as Nelson Eddy, David Bowie.

Julian Who's Nelson Eddy? Don't you like anything at all?

Stephen Look, I like the band, I like the Kinks, Joe Cocker, Merle
Haggard, Billie Holliday, Bessie Smith, George O'Dowd has a
perfectly good voice, Cliff Richard has a perfectly good voice.

Julian Oh! Really!

Stephen Julian, I am not the rock critic for Isis. I am not interested
in the irony of the Velvet Underground as perceived by . . .
Terry Jones. Cliff Richard has a perfectly good voice.

Julian So has David Bowie.

Stephen Yes! I know. So has Nelson fucking Eddy.

Julian You're the most restrictive person I've ever met.
[*Slight pause*]
Who's Nelson Eddy?

Stephen Ask your fucking father when next you have a row. 'This one's
for Brian'.

Julian Don't.

Stephen 'Life like a dome of many coloured glass stains the white
radiance of the Universe.'
[*Pause*]
Come on Julian.
[*Pause*]

Julian The worst time was having to go to bed at seven in the
summer evenings with the light through the curtains. That
was the worst time. The naughtiest boy was called Roebuck.

I always think you're like Roebuck. He kept lizards in his pockets. And he hatched a bird from an egg he'd taken in the woods. They were always beating him for something or scrubbing him up to look angelic. And he never gave in.
[*Pause*]
I don't know what I'd ever do without you. I think I'd just fall apart.
[*Pause*]
Stephen listen, do you think I've got a sense of humour?

Stephen   Of course you have.

Julian   No, honestly.

Stephen   Yes. Tell me that joke.

Julian   Shall I? I'm tired.

Stephen   Come on.

Julian   Do you mean when Roebuck said 'Sir, what's the Latin for hinge?'
[*Laughter*]

Stephen   No.

Julian   Well, when we were out, Roebuck and I, we used to find a telephone box, dial 0 and when the operator answered we used to say 'Is that you operator?' And she'd say 'Yes', and we'd say 'Well, get off the line, there's a train coming'.
[*Laughter*]
Oh, I hate it here.

Stephen   What?

Julian   England. I don't understand it. Let's go to Venice and Florence and Pisa, La Spezia and Viareggio and Leghorn and Rome.

Stephen   Hang on, we haven't been to Lords yet. You said you'd take me to Lords.

Julian   Would you like to go to Lords? It's great at Lords. We could spend the whole day there.

Stephen   Alright. I've been to Rome.

Julian   I've been to Florence. What does that matter? Did you go to the Baths of Caracalla? He wrote 'Prometheus Unbound' in the Baths of Caracalla. Are they beautiful? Listen.
[*Reads*]

'This poem was chiefly written upon the mountainous ruins of the Baths of Caracalla, among the flowery glades, and thickets of odiferous blossoming trees, which are extended in ever winding labyrinths upon its immense platforms and dizzy arches suspended in the air. The bright blue sky of Rome, and the effect of the vigorous awakening spring in that divinest climate, and the new life with which it drenches the spirits even to intoxication, were the inspiration of this drama'.

Stephen	Come on then.
Julian	What?
Stephen	Let's go.
Julian	Stephen.
Stephen	Where did he write 'Epipsychidion'?
Julian	I don't know. Lerici, I suppose.
Stephen	Let's go there then.
Julian	I haven't got any money.
Stephen	I've got money.
Julian	No. I can't take your money. [*Long pause*]
Stephen	You look at me as if I was fucking black magic you know. [JULIAN *sleeps, joint in hand.* PAUL *enters*]
Stephen	Hello.
Paul	You OK? [*Tokes on* JULIAN'*s joint. Picks up book*] Who's reading this?
Stephen	Fuck off.
Paul	[*Laughs*] Are you reading this?
Stephen	Don't.
Paul	Have you been sailing paper boats in the park?
Stephen	Fuck off Paul. [PAUL *gives the joint back to* JULIAN. JULIAN *wakes*]
Julian	Paul . . . is this shirt OK?
Paul	Great. Where d'you get it?

Julian	Do you like it?
Paul	Great. See you later.
	[*Points towards book, laughing*]
Stephen	Fuck off, Paul.
Paul	So long.
	[*Leaving*]
Stephen	Paul.
Paul	What?
Stephen	Fuck off.
Paul	[*Laughing*] Oh, Celia's downstairs.
	[CELIA *enters*]
Celia	Hello.

II

[JULIAN *and* CELIA]

Julian	[*Reading to* CELIA]

Meanwhile, we two will rise, and sit, and walk together,
Under the roof of blue Ionian weather,
And wander in the meadows or ascend
The mossy mountains where the blue heavens bend
With lightest winds, to touch their paramour
Or linger, where the pebble paven shore,
Under the quick, faint kisses of the sea
Trembles and sparkles as with ecstasy . . .
And we will talk, until thought's melody
Becomes too sweet for utterance, and it die
In words, to live again in looks, which dart
With thrilling tone into the voiceless heart,
Harmonising silence without a sound . . .

Isn't that great?

Celia	[*Looking at volume*] I wrote an essay on Epipsychidion when I was at university but I never read it. There was a book out at the time. I cribbed it from that.
Julian	The Pursuit
Celia	I think so.
	[*Pause*]

Julian	Are you having lunch?
Celia	I suppose so.
Julian	Shall we have lunch together? Would you like that?
Celia	Shouldn't we wait?
Julian	I suppose we should. [*Enter* PAUL *and* NELL. *They all greet each other*]
Paul	Where's Stephen?
Julian	Out I should think.
Paul	Where?
Julian	He should be on his way back from the library.
Paul	Shall we go and meet him?
Nell	Yes, is it far?
Paul	No.
Nell	Shall we bicycle?
Paul	No.
Nell	Shall we see you?
Julian	I expect so.
Nell	See you then. [PAUL *and* NELL *go*]
Julian	I don't think Paul likes me.
Celia	Paul!
Julian	Fuck him.
Celia	Is Nell a friend of Paul's?
Julian	I don't know. Look. Come on. Let's go to lunch. I hate crowds, don't you?
Celia	Alright. Where shall we go?
Julian	I know a very nice place. Well, I think it's nice. Do you want to try it?
Celia	Of course. Where is it?
Julian	Holland Park.
Celia	That'll be nice. Where? Oh! That . . . girl's name.

Julian	Yes.
Celia	Where are my keys? [JULIAN *finds them*] What about Stephen?
Julian	Fuck Stephen. [*They start to leave*] Look do you mind if I go and collect some blow first? You don't mind, do you?
Celia	No.
Julian	Do you?
Celia	No. [*Slight pause*]
Julian	Celia. Listen, is this shirt OK?
Celia	Yes. [PAUL *and* NELL *return*]
Nell	We gave up at the front door.
Paul	Nell did. You off somewhere?
Julian	Yes. Is that OK?
Paul	What?
Julian	Is it?
Celia	Come along. Bye bye Paul. [*They say goodbye.* CELIA *and* JULIAN *exit*]
Paul	Here, take this. If I'm seen with Private Eye I'm in trouble.
Nell	With whom?
Paul	With myself. How long before you've got to go?
Nell	Fairly soon.
Paul	You always say that.
Nell	Do I?
Paul	You do. What is it?
Nell	I've never been here before.
Paul	Yes you have.
Nell	Not here.
Paul	How's Keith?

Nell	He's fine, fine. He's fine.
Paul	Is he in town?
Paul	[*Listening – calling*] Stephen! [STEPHEN *enters, carrying books and papers*]
Stephen	Hello. Hello, Nell. Here. [*Gives* PAUL *some magazines*]
Paul	Thanks.
Stephen	They didn't have the London Review of Books so I got Newsline. He loves print. Newsprint. He's the only person I know who says he reads City Limits for the sport. Where's Julian?
Nell	They've . . .
Paul	Haven't seen him.

III

[JULIAN *and* STEPHEN]

Julian	Say.
Stephen	No, I'm not saying. You work it out. Why should I come out with a lot of recriminations? You're happy. Off you go – have a drink – meet whoever – if you didn't want to meet me tonight you just had to say – now – go and meet whoever for whatever reason – you see now I'm doing it. What I didn't want to. I hate you for this. I do. If you apologise once more and don't even follow the apology through with something and then go on apologising I'll . . . I don't mind. I don't want you to change. I'll – I'll just wait for the time when I can say – why did I ever feel this about you. I look and watch and wait for you like a kid outside a pub sitting on the kerb or a step. Tired and waiting and still I wait. And I still wait. And I wait still. Look at the clock on the wall. But I haven't a time to expect you by. But twenty minutes have passed. I go back to my book to read something that makes me look up to see if you've come yet. The noise I've blocked out re-establishes. Glasses. Getting ready for the last haul before time is called. Phone at the other end. Singing has stopped. Clock. Don't look at faces – as I return one red-headed woman gesticulating imposes herself. Crisp packets crackle. Glasses again. The noise is not unpleasant. Bit loud. I look

up, I shall go. Leave you a note saying I've gone. Had you
something more interesting. Wasn't there a half promise. See
you in the. I'll go. Not angry. Or shall I stay? Oh come on. Is it?
No. I know you're not coming. I leave a polite note saying you
bastard.

Julian	Look, I've got to go.
Stephen	Where are you going? I'm sorry. I don't think anyone has ever been so cruel to me ever. So gratuitously. No. Yes. Cruel. They have been I suppose. Ever. Not casually, culpably. Don't apologise. I can't think about it any more. I've managed to survive months of this, I've managed even to survive the red-head with the short stories. But I can't go on unprotected any longer.
Julian	Stephen. Lindy! Stephen.
Stephen	You told me you thought she was very nice. You told me you thought she was very talented.
Julian	Did I? Oh God.
Stephen	And then she sent <u>me</u> the manuscripts.
Julian	I'm not worthy of you. Why don't you just give me up. I'm not worthy of you.
Stephen	You've got some light. Some glow. I find myself crying and you know – I don't even know what it is I'm feeling. I don't know if I'm unhappy or not. I don't even fucking like you. I've located a part of myself in you. And I dread the feeling in the future of my sense of worthlessness now at having been so shallow all the time.
Julian	But you can't let it be like this. Me!
Stephen	Because there has to be a reason to get up in the morning. I have to have some defence.
Julian	Against what?
Stephen	That place.
Julian	Where? Work? Against what?
Stephen	The mendacity. The envy. The fear. The lack of principle. The mismanagement, the lack of vision, the self interest. One's self interest. The atmosphere of witch hunt; the wish to make things worse. The mishandling, the pusillanimity. The unkindness. The lack of any care, the lack of guts to even

stab Caesar when he's dead. 'Speak hands for me'. The trivial nature, the residue of complacency and dissatisfaction and graft. The exhausted ideals, the lack of perspective, the dead wood, the mediocrity, the vaccillation, the meanness of spirit, the gutless, not even opportunism. The terminal air.

Julian   I can't go on with this. I can't go on talking because you . . . such . . . You mustn't. I can't stand it, I can't have it, do you understand? I'd like to bang my head against a wall. If this is about Celia. If you're quizzing me about Celia. There's nothing I can do about it. Do you understand, do you understand? Do you understand? You just want me to be infinitely flexible and you resent my life. You do, Stephen. And you're so very clever at making me feel obscurely guilty and I <u>resent</u> it. I <u>resent</u> it. I'm tired. I haven't got the same emotional stamina as you!

Stephen   You selfish little bastard. It's not emotional stamina. You're a coward. You're tired because you're doped out and you're a coward.

Julian   Leave me alone. I'm wrecked. I've got a headache.

Stephen   You have no strength, you're a fucking coward. It's weakness. You're just weak. 'Just give me some space for a minute – space–give me space. I need space. You don't allow me my space. I have to have space OK'. Sixties doped out nonsense like that. Don't apologise – you're like a drunk. And if you're going to get as stoned as you were last night. There comes a point when one can't have any more to say to you.

Julian   Do you think you were sent by God to change me? You make me feel guilty. Why do you look with such reproach?

Stephen   Don't you dare use the word reproachful to me as a reproach. What you're saying is if I look reproachful you don't like it. I'll punish you . I'll hold it against you , you say. I want something – you really can't give it. You make me feel hopeless, hopeless, hopeless, hopeless, hopeless, hopeless. What you're saying is I'm tired mummy . I'm tired. You perceive a look as a reproach. You don't like reproach and you say I'm tired. I'm going fucking mad. I hear something on the radio and I laugh because it's going to be something I like and I think got you, you bastard . Then I feel the pain of wanting to share it with you – pain that you wouldn't really want to . . . and then I feel I can't sustain the hate – the feeling current in me is too weak and the tears start and then, to cap it all, before our next programme they play Schubert's Seligkeit. Do you remember when I was a character witness over your driving offence? And I thought in that awful court if I was in jail you'd forget to come or come late. I'd look at the clock and five, ten, fifteen minutes late you'd be. Then awkward. It will be time to go. I used to like love songs. Now they have no meaning. Sentimental songs have to be pretty good now.

Julian	We don't ever have any fun any more. You're depressed anyway. That's OK. Don't worry.
Stephen	Well then, let's say goodbye. No. Come on. In that case don't let's fuck about. Just tell me to fuck off.
Julian	No. Come on Stephen. Don't be stupid.
Stephen	Shake hands with me. Come on.
Julian	No.
Stephen	We both seem to be determined to be ourselves to our mutual disadvantage. And let no one think they are protecting me by any hole in the corner affair, when what they are protecting is something quite else.
Julian	It's not you, it's . . .
Stephen	The man Celia's going out with? That aging television man who irons his jeans?
Julian	I feel I'm locked in a tennis court and people keep serving balls to me and I have to play and I can't compete.
Stephen	But you do compete. You've put me in this tennis court.
Julian	Look, this isn't flippant, she's captured my heart.
Stephen	I think you only exist by hurting. Being hurt . . . I can talk.
Julian	Look, I've got to go. Don't despair.
Stephen	Despair? Despair! Despair's OK. It's anxious despair I don't like.
Julian	I don't exist for you Stephen, really. You'd like to blow me out.
Stephen	Do you know, we don't know who the other is.
Julian	I do. I know who you are.

Stephen	But if what you say is true, and I expect it is. You're forgetting I do care! I honestly do!
Julian	And me.
Stephen	You're forgetting. Try as I can, I'm not as immoral as you are.
Julian	Oh, don't moralise, Stephen.
Stephen	Sorry. Sorry.
Julian	Look, I've got to go. I'm really tired. And I've got to be up. I really have. I've got to get myself into shape. I've got to go for a run. Is it OK?
Stephen	Don't give Celia my love.

IV

[CELIA *with flowers in a pretty china jug.*]

Celia	[*Calling*] Are you alright, Julian? [*Pause*] These are lovely. Look how they've lasted. [*Pause*] Julian, have you seen Florence? [*Listening*] Fine. Happy. Happy . . . [*Calls to her cats*] Chloë . . . baby, baby . . . Florence . . .

V

[STEPHEN *and* PAUL]
[STEPHEN *drinking.* PAUL *enters*]

Paul	What's this then?
Stephen	I'm alright.
Paul	What's this then? [*Picking up a bottle of pills*] What are these? Where did you get these? OK?
Stephen	Terrible.
Paul	Is it?
Stephen	It's terrible. Can I come into your bed?

Paul   I expect so.

Stephen   I'm going to kill him. I'm going to fucking kill him. I'll knife him. Please can I come in with you? Where can I get a shooter?

Paul   What do you want a shooter for?

Stephen   I'm going to shoot him.

Paul   Oh. OK. But I don't know where you can get a shooter.

Stephen   Someone must know.

Paul   Nobody I know.

Stephen   I'm going to kill him.

Paul   What is it?

Stephen   It's the anger. And the – anger. It's <u>terrible</u>.

Paul   He takes up with a dislocated Liverpudlian who hit the Hippie trail and who talks about Tibet and anarchy. He goes down West Indian clubs which he calls shebeens; plays pool in the George Canning. He can play two chords of 'The Wild Rover' on his guitar. He has the street wisdom of his mother's housekeeper. Why do you want to kill a figure of fun? He loves black music. Reggae. Ska. Scratch. Hip-hop. He really thinks, somehow, it brings black and white together. It's no different. Jazz. Rhythm'n'blues. Tamla Motown. People have always liked a black man with a banjo.

Stephen   Don't be vulgar Paul.

Paul   Look. You can't . . . He may genuinely like the music, right? But these street acquaintances . . . The only reparation being made is to himself. And it does no good for him, with his nervous off-accent in a mini-cab to West Indian drivers who want honky out of the car as soon as possible. They still fucking hate in the same way I do. Look at the drugs. Look at the hypocrisy surrounding drugs. They say they're after the pushers. They only get the middle men who depend on the Julians. The poor fucking . . . But they won't jail Julian.

Stephen   You smoke dope Paul.

Paul   Yeah, I know.

Stephen   Why are you so angry with him?

Paul   I think perhaps because I'm jealous.

Stephen   Why?

Paul   I think I must hate something he stands for in you. Have you
ever seen him spray his yucca? The yucca . . . And Shelley . . ?
Whatever happened to Blake? They used to arrogate poor
Blake in my day. Oh I don't know . . .

Stephen   It's because in the beginning there was no-one else
in the frame. He knew no-one. Because all this street
acquaintanceship is so very touching. And because he
was alone. Or rather he felt abandoned. He can't tell the
difference between being alone and being abandoned.

Paul   You mean you can't Stephen.

Stephen   It's the pure filament of self-obsession.

Paul   Come on. He's not worth it.

Stephen   What do you mean, he's not worth it? Of course he's not
worth it. Who is worth it? Worth it. I know he's not worth it.
He knows he's not worth it. And it's dawned on you he's not
worth it. Worth it!

He really doesn't have a life – he really is still only a string
of appetites. Some of which he can satisfy. Oh he's weaker
than I am. He has no, no, no, understanding of other people.
When he says he doesn't gossip, it's because he doesn't have
any interest in anyone. When he is interested it's because
someone has been kind to him. He's like a light bulb. Lights
up no matter who pulls the switch. Stick with it, I say. Don't
see him. Don't project your future loss. But what am I going
to do for the rest of the evening?

He can't reciprocate even a desire for a friendship. Although
he seems to want to, and to an extent needs to define himself
by me. I even dislike him. He is callow and yet sweet natured –
or, at least, what is charming about him indicates sweetness
and warmth. We went to the Bacon exhibition. He can't
bear human images. Bare figures against a plain background.
Couldn't understand. What is it in Keats? He can't live
without an irritable reaching after fact and reason. Some of
the figures he understood, but he saw them as businessmen.
Politicians. Things to hate. Oh!

What's the opposite of negative capability? Positive incapacity. I lack almost entirely that objectivity which is supposed, by some, to be the prerequisite of being an artist.

Paul   Look Steve . . .

Stephen   I don't want a suitable love object. I just want revenge on a couple of people, frankly. He's fucking Celia. He's in love with Celia.

Paul   Everyone's in love with Celia.

Stephen   Are you in love with Celia?

Paul   No.

Stephen   You fucked her.

Paul   I have not.

Stephen   What's wrong with Celia? Ring this number. If Celia answers put the phone down.

Paul   It's an ansaphone. What does that mean?

Stephen   Nothing. He sent her fucking flowers. Ring this number.

Paul   Christ! Steve . . . No answer.

Stephen   Oh . . . God. Roses. I think I was a very loving child and never grew out of it.

Paul   Come on. Let's go down.

Stephen   No, I'm OK.

VI

[NELL *drying her hair.*]

Nell   Darling!
                [*Pause*]
                What time's your train?
                [*Pause*]
                Keith, damn!
                [*Her hair tangles*]
                Keith. What time's your train? Want a lift?
                [*Pause*]
                OK.

VII

[CELIA *and* PAUL]

Paul   Do you know what he's doing to himself?

Celia   No. What do you mean?

Paul   What do you think I mean?
[*Emptying pills violently on to the floor*]
You live four streets away, Celia. He won't do anything but sleep.

Celia   You know Stephen!

Paul   Stephen? I know Stephen.

Celia   Look Paul, I'm sorry, he'll have to put up with it. I didn't mean that. Oh! He's alright, isn't he?

Paul   Celia. I never thought you were stupid. What is it? You look as if this was the love of your life. Is it? I hope it is.

Celia   Why?

Paul   This smug radiance had better be worth it.

Celia   Why?

Paul   It's on the cards I think. It really is. He's going to do something Celia only not, apparently, intentionally.

Celia   But you're keeping an eye on him, aren't you?

Paul   I never took you for a hard girl either. How is Golden Boy? Have you taught him to play bridge? I hope he's a better partner than you are.

Celia   Paul. Stephen's, I owe . . .

Paul   Your fucking job to Stephen.

Celia   But Stephen's. Well, <u>you</u> know Stephen.

Paul   Look Celia. What are you saying? What? What? I do know Stephen. What's Golden Boy think he's doing? He's a real beauty he is. A real fucking sleeping beauty. He's like a dum-dum bullet, and what do you mean . . . Oh, I'm going.

Celia   Paul, I'm sorry Paul. What about these, Paul?

Paul   I'm leaving them for Golden Boy.

VIII

[STEPHEN *alone*]
[JULIAN *enters carrying a record set*]

Stephen	Hello.
Julian	I've come to see you. Is it OK?
Stephen	Yeah, yeah. How are you?
Julian	I'm alright.
Stephen	What's that — FIDELIO! Julian! Where'd you get it?
Julian	Fuck off.
Stephen	Sorry. Where'd you get it? Is this for me?
Julian	No. Yes it is for you.
Stephen	Where did you get it? Did Celia give you this?
Julian	Yes.
Stephen	Yes. Her last boyfriend was a musician. I suppose the next one will get a copy of the Oxford Book of Romantic Verse. I'm sorry . . . I'm sorry.
Julian	No, no, no it's OK.
Stephen	Are you staying?
Julian	Can I?
Stephen	Of course.
Julian	For a bit, I'll have to go later. Is it alright?
Stephen	Of course.
Julian	Stephen, why haven't I seen you?
Stephen	Julian!
Julian	Why are you laughing? What did I say? What is it?
Stephen	It's alright, it's alright.
Julian	You know I don't care for her half as much as I care for you.
Stephen	This is really fucking awful.
Julian	What is?

Stephen	It's just I can't bear the thought of someone knowing more about you than me.
Julian	She doesn't know more about me than you, nobody knows more about me than you. I don't know more about me than you.
Stephen	Why are you doing this?
Julian	I don't know.
Stephen	There's a pullover of yours in there.
Julian	Is there?
Stephen	I've been wearing it, do you mind?
Julian	No.
Stephen	Because it smells of you. Pathetic isn't it? Have you seen Fidelio?
Julian	No.
Stephen	Have you listened to it?
Julian	No.
Stephen	Have you been to the opera?
Julian	Yes.
Stephen	What did you see?
Julian	Der Rosenkavalier.
Stephen	Did you like it?
Julian	No.
Stephen	Quite right. [*Whistles*] 'Hab mir's gelobt, ihn lieb zu haben auf der richtigen Weis, Daß ich selbst seine Lieb zu einer andern Noch lieb hab! Hab mir freilich nicht gedacht, daß es so bald mir auferlegt sollt werden!' [JULIAN *sleeps*]
Julian	What's that?
Stephen	Rosenkavalier.
Julian	What's Fidelio about?
Stephen	Well, there's . . .

Julian   No. No, no. What's it about?

Stephen   It's about freedom and constancy. You should know about that.

Julian   What's Der Rosenkavalier about?

Stephen   Julian! You've seen it.

Julian   I know.

Stephen   It's about nothing.

Julian   Is it good?

Stephen   Very good.

Julian   Which is the best? Is Fidelio <u>very</u> good?

Stephen   <u>Very, very</u> good.

Julian   Yes, I thought it might be. I didn't like Der Rosenkavalier. I don't like the fucking opera, do you?

Stephen   Yes. No. I dunno. I don't go. No.

Julian   Is Der Rosenkavalier good?

Stephen   Very good.

Julian   I don't understand anything.

Stephen   Come on.

Julian   Stephen.

Stephen   You'd better go.

Julian   Stephen.

Stephen   Shall I call you a cab?

Julian   Yes, I'd better go.

Stephen   You're such . . . There's a towel of yours in there as well, and half a bottle of JoJoba, and the Eucryl smoker's, and a pair of swimming trunks, and a tube of Daktarin, and the African fucking honey, and the Eau du Portugal.

Julian   That's OK.

Stephen   And a packet of three with one to go.
                [JULIAN *has left the recording of Fidelio.*]

IX

[CELIA *and* JULIAN]

Celia	Are you alright?
Julian	Fine.
Celia	What is it?
Julian	I'm alright, honestly. You?
Celia	Not very. Are we going?
Julian	Don't you want to?
Celia	Not really.
Julian	Don't let's go then. [*Pause*] What is it Cels? You've been like this for hours. What've I done?
Celia	Nothing. Honestly. Let's stop. Let's stop it.
Julian	Something . . .
Celia	You can't accommodate to anybody, can you?
Julian	What?
Celia	Everybody must accommodate to you.
Julian	What? Christ! Christ! What? To me? Who's been doing the accommodating if I haven't been doing the accommodating?
Celia	Alright.
Julian	It isn't alright. Oh no, it isn't alright. It isn't, alright. Oh no. Everything you want to do, I do. I meet your friends. I go to restaurants with people you like. I go to concerts because you like them. I spend my time here. You haven't even visited my flat.
Celia	I have.
Julian	Once. My friends. All I did was not go to your parents for the weekend. That's all, Celia. It isn't alright.
Celia	I didn't mind you not coming for the weekend.
Julian	You minded.
Celia	I didn't. I'm perfectly satisfied with my parents. I can't help it if my father's a school inspector and my mother's a teacher. I can't help it if you don't like them.

Julian	I don't know if I like them or if I dislike them, anyway. There's no reason for me to like them.
Celia	Or dislike them.
Julian	I don't. I don't know them. I don't want to know them. All this cosiness. I don't want to see them or visit them, or walk the dogs. Any of that nonsense . I don't want to know mummy or daddy. This is enough. Quite enough.
Celia	Julian!
Julian	Quite enough. Quite enough. Quite enough.

X

[STEPHEN *and* JULIAN]

Stephen	Will I see you later? Oh no.
Julian	Why not.
Stephen	You've got to have dinner with Celia haven't you?
Julian	That's tomorrow night.
Stephen	It isn't.
Julian	Isn't it? Where's her note? Christ, it is tonight. Oh God I'm so tired. I think it's glandular fever. Stephen. Do you think? Listen do you think I've got glandular fever? She says can we meet where no one can gawp. Really who's interested in people gawping? Anyway, I'll have to go won't I? Perhaps I'll just go for a drink. I'll ring her, we'll just go for a drink. What do you think? I'll have to have a shower.
Stephen	Listen. I can't say anything. You go for a drink. I think there's something grotesque about this, anyway.
Julian	Isn't this how you do these things?
Stephen	I don't know.
Julian	Oh Christ, I haven't got any money and I haven't got my cheque book. Do you think it matters?
Stephen	No. Look you'll have to pay. I've got thirty quid. Do you want it?
Julian	Can I have twenty-five?

XI

[STEPHEN *and* JULIAN]

Stephen	What is it?
Julian	Nothing.
Stephen	What's the matter?
Julian	Leave me alone.
Stephen	What is it?
Julian	I'm in trouble.
Stephen	What trouble? Oh God.
Julian	What? No.
Stephen	What then?
Julian	She gave me a lift home and when we got there she started crying.
Stephen	Why?
Julian	I asked her how the cats were.
Stephen	How were they? Didn't one of them bite you once?
Julian	Yes. Florence.
Stephen	Christ.
Julian	I made her come in, and we talked for hours and hours and hours and hours till two in the morning. She went home. Then I felt sorry for her and myself and went over there. What am I going to do now?
Stephen	I don't know Julian.
Julian	She says she fought hard for her independence. Fuck her. I dreamt I was in a desert in America and you deserted me. I suppose you will. Won't you . . . ?

XII

[CELIA *and* PAUL]

Celia	It's when you can't change anything. I've tried, I've not been able to. I've only made it worse. Will you tell him for me, that he must or I'll die. How stupid, will you speak to him? Oh . . . Will you please?

Paul	Celia . . .
Celia	No. He's . . .
Paul	Yes. He's not much use to you is he? Is he?
Celia	He's left nothing. This for a little love. This for that. And yes . . . No. Oh I hope I never have to see him again. I do. I do. I do. I won't come out. Do you mind?
Paul	Celia.
Celia	I must go to work on Monday. I haven't been to work for two weeks. But I can't stay off any longer. I haven't seen anyone. Please you won't tell him I've spoken to you, will you?
Paul	Of course I won't. Come on Celia.
Celia	No. I'll stay in. Thanks. Thanks.

XIII

[JULIAN *and* STEPHEN]

Julian	You know that girl? That tall girl? I think she was flirting with me.
Stephen	Don't. Please don't. Don't. By every bloody thing, don't.
Julian	Why not? Why not? Can't I?
Stephen	Look, she lives with a very nice bloke. Just don't.
Julian	What's his name?
Stephen	Keith. I've never met him.
Julian	She asked me if I was having an affair with you.
Stephen	Aye, she would. Are you? That's why she was flirting with you.
Julian	Is it? Really, is it? Do you like her?
Stephen	I don't really know her.
Julian	It's alright. She won't like me, those kind of girls never do. What's she like?
Stephen	She's a hockey field Venus. Half good looking like you. Grew too tall to be a dancer, I shouldn't wonder. They live in Cambridge in one of those big houses on the Chesterton Road and her aunt was Wittgenstein's doctor's receptionist,

or north Oxford and their mother was an actress, but gave
it up to have nine brutally concerned children. Or she lopes
along Chiswick Mall, the daughter of a judge. And gives you
pebbles or driftwood for Christmas. Trouble. Take a very long
spoon. I bet she was at the Band Aid concert.

Julian   She told me there's a very good double bill at the Rio in
Dalston. And that restaurant on Newington Green.

Stephen   Yes. I suppose the return match'll be at the Ritzy in Brixton.

Julian   No. She's . . . Keith? She's a terrible flirt.
[*Pause*]
Am I only half good looking?

Two

I

[JULIAN *and* NELL *drinking white wine*]

Julian	[*Reading*] Our breath shall intermix, our bosoms bound,

And our veins beat together; and our lips
With other eloquence than words, eclipse
The soul that burns between them, and the wells
Which boil under our being's inmost cells,
The fountains of our deepest life, shall be
Confused in Passion's golden purity . . .
We shall become the same, we shall be one
Spirit within two frames . . .
One hope within two wills, one will beneath
Two overshadowing minds, one life, one death,
One Heaven, one Hell, one immortality,
And one annihilation . . .

Isn't it great?

Nell   It's like making love.

Julian   Is it?

Nell   Do you want some of this?

Julian   Thanks.

Nell   What is it?

Julian   I'm restless.

Nell   Oh.

Julian   Not with you. I don't know what I'm doing. Work. Everything. I'm a sort of displaced person. I feel like some sort of refugee here.

Nell   How? Come on. Because you were born abroad. Really?

Julian   That I suppose. A result of feeling that school was where they called home and home was in Malaya and now I don't know where I am.

Nell   Why don't you go back?

Julian	I'd like to. I'd love to.
Nell	I've never been very far . . . Elba.
Julian	Oh, Malaya . . . oh, you should.
Nell	What are you laughing at?
Julian	Thinking of here and there.
Nell	Where were you born?
Julian	Kuala Lumpur. But mainly I think of the Cameron Highlands house.
Nell	Not a plantation? Really?
Julian	Really.
Nell	How very glamorous. I can see how you feel as you do. Though I like where we live. Where I was born, in fact.
Julian	Where?
Nell	North. On the Borders. There is something utterly strange and beautiful and compelling about Border Country I think . . . I went to Wales once and we got to somewhere out of Shakespeare . . . Mortimer's Cross. And I got this feeling, scary. Beautiful. I expected Red Indians. But our Borders . . .
Julian	Do you go home?
Nell	I love going home. In spite of . . . Mainly for the place. The village. The town. Our house and when we're all together I suppose.
Julian	In spite of what? What does your father do?
Nell	He's a doctor. He's a consultant, in fact. Mainly in Newcastle. But sometimes in Edinburgh and even London. But he won't move here. He likes the North and the Scots, though he's very English. We all went to boarding schools in the South and my brother went to public school here. You must come. My mother likes visitors and us all there. Though I don't like her very much.
Julian	Why?
Nell	Well, of course I do. But. What is it about Malaya? Is it like India? How they write about it. Is it like that?
Julian	Yes. Longing. But it's everything, the people.

Nell	Did you have an ayah? No, that's India.
Julian	Yes, we had an amah. She was called an amah. My favourite had to leave – to go back to her village. It's just everything. The green. England! The green in Malaya. I'm sure where you live is beautiful. We used to go to Scotland. But there. Everything. The rain. I stood in the rain once and my parents were rowing inside. I ran off the verandah and into the rain. The rain was just soaking me. English rain is so hateful somehow. Mean. Untrustworthy. Cold.
Nell	What did your father do before he retired?
Julian	Not as romantic as you think but yes, tea. After the war he worked for a company in Penang and then Kuala Lumpur. He met my mother there. They aren't grand, you know. My mother comes from Southampton.
Nell	I'm sure there must be grand people even in Southampton.
Julian	He was commissioned in the war. And then after was very hard-working and enterprising and clever and competitive.
Nell	Was it his plantation?
Julian	No. [*Laughs*] He worked for a company. Later a huge American multinational company. He ended up Chairman of one of their subsidiaries back in Kuala Lumpur. He's loaded. I know he hates it here. More than me. He won't say. He was very big in the emergency. Not back in the army. But I don't know . . . being important . . . holding civilians together. Of course he thinks things have gone from bad to worse, which of course they have. Do you play Mah Jong?
Nell	What? No.
Julian	My father and mother and their Sussex friends actually play Mah Jong. He's, oh Christ, it's impossible. He's bright, I know he is. But he's so competitive. He knows the truth. I think he's lost his soul. My parents don't deserve a better chronicler than Somerset Maugham. They really don't.
Nell	Are you like him?
Julian	No, I'm not!
Nell	Alright, angel, come on.
Julian	I look like my mother. She's pretty despicable, I'm afraid. She's vain and weak and spoiled. Is that bad of me? His temper I have, I suppose. No, I don't. You?

Nell	I can cope with my father, but I hate him for putting up with my mother. I hate her quite passionately really. Maybe because she'd had this man for years and my father knows. And her daunting competence I hate. I like my sisters and especially my brother, of course.
Julian	What's he called?
Nell	Giles.
Julian	Do you want a smoke?
Nell	Look, I should go.
Julian	Don't go.
Nell	Look, this isn't supposed to be on. I've got to see Keith before he leaves, though I'm fed up with him at the moment, actually.
Julian	That's between you and Keith.
Nell	Are you having an affair with Stephen?
Julian	You keep asking that. Does it look like I am?
Nell	Look, my brother's gay.
Julian	So is mine. Or at least that's what he just told his wife.
Nell	Giles, when he was at public school. I was always jealous of his romances.
Julian	Really.
Nell	He was once in love with someone called John Graham and he, John Graham, threw Giles over for someone called Philip Richards and Giles was so angry. So angry, he made himself ill, and he took two aspirins and was in the sanatorium for three days. He said it was my mother and I think it even was my mother. But it wasn't, it was John Graham. And that's how he got John Graham back. And when he, John Graham, left school, he came back during the term and took Giles out in his motor car. I thought it was incredible. I still do. Exciting.
Julian	Not for Philip Richards I should think. Do you want a smoke? Do you smoke?
Nell	Sometimes.
Julian	Have a smoke.
Nell	OK. I'll ring Keith. Then I'll read something to you.

II

[STEPHEN, JULIAN *and* PAUL]

Julian	I'm going out.
Stephen	Don't go out. Come on. Sit down. What's the thing about one of your friends that you most like to remember?
Paul	I don't know.
Stephen	I know what it is about you.
Paul	What?
Stephen	In the other house I was sitting on the sofa by the fire, reading Great Expectations, and there was a soft tread on the step and a light tap on the door, and in you came and you said 'Miss Barrett, Miss Barrett, I've come to take you away'.
Julian	Look, I've got to go out.
Stephen	Don't go out.
Julian	I'm fucking going out to get some stuff, OK? OK Paul?
Stephen	Don't. Come on. [JULIAN *exits*]
Stephen	Oh, Christ.
Paul	A thing to hate. The public school as an image of England. They can take the slipper these boys but they don't know how to put their dukes up. And instead of going in the army where they belong, they persecute the rest of us.
Stephen	Oh don't Paul.
Paul	I was in college with someone who went home at the end of the winter term and his parents had moved without leaving an address. There are families and families, Julian.
Stephen	Young people are like unborn babies. It's the fate of each generation to have the young express themselves in different ways. Flappers. Teddy Boys. Flower children. Skinheads. And the old must put up with it. To me they look like unborn babies. Spoiled. I spoiled it. Seeking more. Not accepting the unfinished edge of things. Not letting it drift as it will. And put the effort in when it's needed. But why can't he say..? Why can't he show..?
Paul	He can't because he's like that. And you'll have to put up with it or ship out.

Stephen	What am I to do! I can't just drop him. I don't want to. Shall I give him up?
Paul	Yes. And what will you do then? You're addicted to him. It's an addiction.
Stephen	What do you know about Nell?
Paul	When she left school she did something first. She didn't go to Cambridge straight away, I know. She wouldn't I think. What was it? I don't think it was the VSO.
Stephen	I bet it was VSO.
Paul	Nor the National Youth Theatre.
Stephen	It must have been one or the other. It must have been. I bet she played Helena. God, Vanessa Redgrave's got a lot to answer for, except perhaps her politics. Have you ever seen her? She's like a less subtly violent Nell. I bet Nell's shadowly concerned.
Paul	I think she's fantastic. She burns me.
Stephen	Who, Nell?
Paul	No. Nell . . . Well . . . She has, Stephen, in her time.
Stephen	But she isn't twenty-four anymore.
Paul	I'd give her one.
Stephen	You've given her one. [PAUL *laughs*]
Paul	How was it at the weekend?
Stephen	Home?
Paul	Yeah. Your mother OK?
Stephen	No. I think I'm too much bother for her now. I think my concern makes her even more agitated.
Paul	Is she in for long this time?
Stephen	I don't know. She just sits there and suddenly her eyes light up. I seem inevitably to be caught up in a passionate and romantic attachment for someone who needs you but doesn't want you. It's like an article in one of your magazines down there. The children on YOP schemes. Young boys joining the army. Brothers and brothers-in-law in and out of work. We went over to Cardiff for a meal. My younger sister, Kath, she's like a sans-culottes. We had to wait for a taxi for hours because she

	wouldn't go with the firm that took the blacklegs to Merthyr Vale. She says they're killers by implication.
Paul	Aren't they?
Stephen	My father says – 'I tell you, Stephen, I'm glad I'm not a young man. It's worse than the thirties. I tell you Stephen, in 1926 when I was a shop-steward'. I never knew he was a shop-steward, he never told me he was a shop-steward. 'We couldn't get two fellers to come out on strike and we warned them, and when we went back the manager sacked them'. He could have only been twenty-four in '26. 'You in work, Stephen? How's work? When you going back?'
Paul	Yeah. Neurotic symptoms in the upper working class. Routledge Keegan Paul. It comes to something when your happiest times was when your mother went to put flowers on her father's grave. Playing in the long grass. Playing and watching. Pleasant like another child would watch its mother knitting. No tears. Sunny day. Come here. There we are. Beautiful grasses. Secretly I think my father would be relieved if I voted Tory. I think it would be proof that I'd done something. But we seemed to have moved class without breaking faith with chaos.
Stephen	I don't know about my father – if I voted Tory it would be the only thing that would bring my mother out of the mental hospital. There was this play and a man on a park bench and he said; 'I feel I haven't been part of life'. Just like the Cherry Orchard. Something like that. Have you been part of life?
Paul	I don't know what that means.
Stephen	It goes through one I suppose in its own way. If we will let life live us instead of being afraid or thinking other lives should be our lives. It's our own life we must live.
Stephen	The new cruelties are the old ones, you know. The new respectability is just the grasping for individual freedom by a safe majority so they destroy individuals weaker than themselves. The loneliness of all those people lonely. They'd be less unhappy if they knew they were just lonely. Loneliness of the summer evenings of family life. The winter evening of after football. That rancourous mean-spirited arguing about sport. De-dum de-dum de-dum de-dum. Partick Thistle. Heart of Midlothian. Queen of the South. The loneliness not knowing it. The

chocolate swiss roll. My brother's football gear. My sisters arguing. Alone. Among them. Chewing gum under the table stuck to my trousers. Iron it out. The loneliness. Dusk 4.30, winter. That sigh from her. That sigh. That snore from him.

[JULIAN *enters*]

Julian	Hello.
Stephen	Alright?
Julian	Yeah. Do you want some of this Paul?
Paul	Aye.

III

[JULIAN *and* STEPHEN]

Stephen	What is it?
Julian	Nothing.
Stephen	Fuck it Julian. You were all over me half an hour ago. What is it?
Julian	You're the last person I should tell.
Stephen	Then if I'm the last person you should tell. Why are you pulling this? When you look like this you're either dying or angry or frightened.
Julian	Well, if I look like this why don't you take the hint and leave me alone?
Stephen	Alright.
Julian	I'm fucking furious.
Stephen	Why?
Julian	I can't Stephen.
Stephen	Oh Christ, why am I putting myself through this. I don't know what to do – is it a test? What is it? You make me feel nothing. I'm nothing. I'm so ashamed of this. Half an hour ago . . . This is wrong. Being with you makes me feel like a woman with none of the compensations, and I don't like it. This being controlled by a boy. Nobody can win with you, can they?
Julian	I'm not competing.
Stephen	You say I'm in competition with you. That's because if somebody puts an experience of theirs up against yours –

then you think it somehow robs you. I'm not trying to. At least I don't think I am. Oh God.
[*Pause*]
Come on Julian.

Julian	I asked her out and at the last minute she changed her mind.
Stephen	Who? Oh God.
Julian	She said she had to see Keith. Why did she do that?
Stephen	Well, mm. Hang on. [*Moves away, hand to his mouth*] It's alright. Oh, Julian. They do live together.
Julian	Sometimes.
Stephen	Well, I don't know. This is like being under the guillotine.
Julian	Ah. Fuck it. I'm fed up with this. Nothing gonna come of this. It's alright, you're alright, we're alright. I'm going to ring her and tell her to fuck off. Oh, she won't be there.
Stephen	Leave a message on her ansaphone.
Julian	She hasn't got an ansaphone.
Stephen	Of course she's got an ansaphone. All your girlfriends have ansaphones. They're like iron lungs to them. What colour are her eyes?
Julian	Er . . .
Stephen	What colour are my eyes? Don't look.
Julian	Grey. I can talk about her mouth if you like.
Stephen	I always knew you thought a woman's place was on her knees with a mouthful of cock.
Julian	Stephen.
Stephen	Julian.
Julian	I wish I'd never met her. But I like her. She likes you.
Stephen	Thanks.
Julian	Do you like her?
Stephen	I don't really know her. I can see why you like her.
Julian	She's kind.
Stephen	You mean she's classier than Celia. She won't make you feel so parvenu.
Julian	Is she better than me?

Stephen	Oh! No.
Julian	Ah fuck her.
Stephen	It's alright. [STEPHEN *exits*]
Julian	Stephen, is she better looking than me?
Stephen	What? [STEPHEN *returns*]
Julian	It's alright.
Stephen	It's alright. Sick. Here, this must be Nell's brooch. She left it in the bathroom.

IV

[NELL *chasing* JULIAN]

Julian	No no no. Here. [*Giving her some flowers*] Don't.
Nell	Thanks! Oh . . . they're beautiful.
Julian	Do you love me?
Nell	What?
Julian	I do. [NELL *laughs*] No!
Nell	They're beautiful! Do you love me?
Julian	With all my heart. You?
Nell	'I love you with so much of my heart that I have nothing left to give.'
Julian	Where's that from?
Nell	Aha! Got you! These really are beautiful. You have one.
Julian	I can't carry a rose.
Nell	Come on.
Julian	No.
Nell	Come on.
Julian	No
Nell	Oh
Julian	Oh. What is it?
Nell	I suppose we shouldn't . . . [*Pause*] Stephen's in this, isn't he? Isn't he?

Julian	No. Well, people are in everything, aren't they? Have you had a holiday?
Nell	Yes.
Julian	I haven't.
Nell	Oh, poor boy.
Julian	Don't.
Nell	Come on. Oh!
Julian	What? What is it? [NELL *begins to cry*] Don't. [*Goes to her*]
Nell	Don't. Keith's coming back. And then he's coming to town to live properly.
Julian	That isn't a proper thing to discuss.
Nell	Isn't it? Must we only discuss what you want to discuss?
Julian	No. Don't be angry.
Nell	Anyway, things will have to take their course.
Julian	I'll wait, you know, for as long as it takes.
Nell	Are we going to lunch?
Julian	Yes. What . . . what are you doing this afternoon?
Nell	Work.
Julian	I'm damn well taking the afternoon off.
Nell	That's rather irresponsible.
Julian	Can you take the afternoon off?
Nell	I can . . . but I won't.
Julian	Come on. Come on.
Nell	Haven't you had a holiday really?
Julian	No. Where did you go?
Nell	We went to Spain. Fantastic. What is it? Well, we did go. Where . . . where are you going?
Julian	Oh. The Maldives or . . . I want to go to Italy. I was going with Stephen. He won't come.
Nell	When?

Julian	In a couple of weeks. I'm not going alone. I'm not going without you. Will you come?
Nell	All right.
Julian	Will you? <u>Will</u> you? I'll get the tickets. I'll do the hotel. I know, I'll hire a car.
Nell	Where?
Julian	We'll fly to Pisa and drive to the bay of Viareggio. It'll be great . . . [*Pause*] What about . . . ?
Nell	I'll handle that. And Stephen?
Julian	I've told you. <u>Will</u> you take the afternoon off?
Nell	Wear this and I might. [*Gives him a rose*]

V

[PAUL *and* STEPHEN]

Paul	Coming for a drink?
Stephen	Aye. Ok.
Paul	Do you want to wait for Boy Blue?
Stephen	No.
Paul	We'll wait.
Stephen	No.
Paul	We'll wait.
Stephen	No. [JULIAN *enters carrying a Paul Smith carrier bag*]
Paul	We don't have to wait.
Stephen	We're going for a drink.
Julian	No, I've got to pack.
Stephen	Come for a pint.
Julian	No. A pint. Oh no. Fuck it.
Stephen	What is it?
Julian	I've lost my driving licence. [*Violently*] I've got an international bloody driver's licence and I don't know where it is!

Paul	I'm going for a drink then, OK?
Stephen	Hang on. Well, where can it be?
Julian	I don't know.
Paul	See you in the pub.
Stephen	Hang on, Paul.
Julian	I'll ring home, it may be there.
Paul	So long.
Stephen	Hang on. It'll be there.
Paul	I'm going. [*Exits*]
Stephen	Paul!
Julian	I don't want to go.
Stephen	It'll be great. You'll meet people.
Julian	Here. [*Gives him the bag*]
Stephen	What's . . . !
Julian	You wanted it. [*Takes out a shirt*]
Stephen	What? Julian, the money.
Julian	Do you like it? Do you? Do you really like it?
Stephen	It's the most expensive shirt I've ever had.
Julian	Do you really like it? Do you? Is it OK?
Stephen	Great. I'll put it on.
Julian	Oh Christ. I've got to go. I've got to go home for the weekend and then Gatwick on Monday. Oh God.
Stephen	It'll be alright. Take them something.
Julian	I've got something.
Stephen	And keep your mouth shut.
Julian	OK.
Stephen	Hear me.
Julian	Yeah.
Stephen	Do you hear me?
Julian	Alright. I'll ring you from the airport before the flight takes off.
Stephen	You won't, Julian.
Julian	I will.
Stephen	How can you?
Julian	I'll ring you.
Stephen	Will you?

Julian	I promise. I've got to go, OK?
Stephen	Have a nice time.
Julian	Shouldn't think so.
Stephen	You will.
Julian	Do you really like the shirt?

VI

[CELIA *and* STEPHEN]

Stephen	[*Off*] He won't be long.
Celia	Fine.
Stephen	[*Off*] He shouldn't be long. [*Pause*] [STEPHEN *enters with a tea tray*] Only teabags.
Celia	That's fine. [STEPHEN *pours tea*]
Stephen	He's usually in by now. Is that him? [*Calling*] Paul! No. [*Pause*] Work OK?
Celia	Great. I've been promoted.
Stephen	Really?
Celia	Yes.
Stephen	Paul didn't say.
Celia	Paul doesn't know. That's partly why I came round. [*Pause*]
Celia	You look well, Stephen.
Stephen	I am well. More?
Celia	No. Thanks. No. Haven't finished this.
Stephen	This is terrible tea. [*She picks up a copy of 'The Face'*]
Celia	Do you read 'The Face'? [*'The Face' is covering the recording of 'Fidelio'*]
Stephen	No I don't read 'The Face'. This tea is really awful. Don't finish it. I'll make some more.

Celia	No. Who's that?
Stephen	[*Listening*] Paul.
Paul	Yeah. [PAUL *enters*]
Stephen	Where have you been?
Paul	What do you mean, where have I been? To work is where I have been. Hello stranger. OK?
Celia	Hello.
Stephen	She's been promoted.
Paul	Have you? I'll get a cup.
Stephen	No. Put the kettle on. This is awful. The water didn't boil.
Paul	OK.
Stephen	No, I'll do it. [STEPHEN *exits*]
Celia	Thank God you've come. I'll have to go
Paul	Why?
Celia	Well.
Paul	Julian? He's in Italy.
Celia	Oh. With whom?
Paul	Himself. Do you care?
Celia	I don't. I don't Paul. Honestly I don't.
Paul	Anyone new? Going out with anyone?
Celia	Paul. Yes, I am actually.
Paul	Really Celia. Your public secrecy. I'm glad about the job.
Celia	Yes.
Stephen	[*Off*] I won't be long.
Celia	Look. I'll have to go. I just wanted to tell you. [STEPHEN *enters*]
Stephen	I made proper tea.
Paul	This domesticity's a bit of a change.
Stephen	Guests.
Celia	None for me. I'm off.

Stephen	Oh. Sure? [*She kisses him. He returns the kiss. She starts to go. He stops her*]
Stephen	You look pretty today, Celia. Well, you always look pretty. But today especially. Must be the job.
Celia	Yes. Bye. I'll let myself out.
Paul	No.
Celia	Really. Bye. [CELIA *exits*]
Stephen	Do you want some tea?
Paul	Yeah.
Stephen	Pour it then will you? I don't want any.

VII

[JULIAN *and* STEPHEN]

Julian	Don't let's go on. It was awful really.
Stephen	Come on. You look great. Was it really awful? No girls? No girls Julian? What about the grove of Catullus?
Julian	Look, Stephen. Look, I can't. It just makes me nervous.
Stephen	OK. You know you said you'd ring from the airport.
Julian	Oh my God. When I got back? I didn't.
Stephen	When you left.
Julian	Did I? Oh . . .
Stephen	Have you rung home?
Julian	No. I haven't rung home.
Stephen	Have you rung anyone?
Julian	Do you mean Nell? Why should I ring Nell? Why shouldn't I ring Nell?
Stephen	I don't know. Tell us about Italy, Julian.
Julian	You know I'm not good with women. She's a friend. Just a friend. Can't I have a friend?
Stephen	Why not? I've got a friend. Thank God for a friend. Thank God for Paul!

Julian	Is he your best friend? Aren't I your best friend? I thought I was your best friend. Nell. I can't act normally as far as she's concerned. She's afraid she's going to hurt you. Celia said you have to get on with it.
Stephen	Infatuation.
Julian	What?
Stephen	Look it up. Go on look it up. You don't need to look it up. I looked it up. It doesn't help. 'Nativity once in the main of light crawls to maturity'. You're like the main of light. Angel. Isn't that what she calls you? Christ Nell. 'While you've a Lucifer to light your fag, smile boys that's the style'.
Julian	You're the most restrictive person I've ever met. She calls me that. Yes. Why not?
Stephen	Because, Golden Boy, It's so obvious.
Julian	I've enough crowding inside my head. I've enough criticising myself. I don't need you crowding and criticising me. Don't say, look at that, look at that, listen to this. You're like, you're like . . . You're endlessly trying to describe me.
Stephen	This is going to end up with one of us dead.
Julian	You'll have friends if anything bad happens.
Stephen	If you had a bit more character you'd have ended up a born-again Christian. I used to love you more than I hated you. Now I hate you. I hate you. Do you know I hate you? I've got to go through with this to learn never to do it again. Never. Never to let it happen to me again. I don't know what to do. You'll have to do something. I'm tired after work and I don't know what to do and it's all my fault, it's so humiliating. Why do I seem to be just letting this humiliation happen? I could kill you. Better than being dead. [*Pause*] You really didn't like anything but the swimming and the food at all. Didn't you go into a church?
Julian	Yes, we went into a church . . .
Stephen	What is it? What's the matter Julian?
Julian	Nothing.
Stephen	Was she Italian?
Julian	I'll kill you if you go on about that holiday.
Stephen	You'd be doing me the greatest of favours.

Julian	Oh come on. You can't say that. Oh Christ. Don't say that.
Stephen	Well. Where's the postcard?
Julian	Would you like it? I didn't post it. [*Gives postcard to* STEPHEN]
Stephen	But there's nothing on it.
Julian	I was lying.
Stephen	I don't care, write on it now. [JULIAN *writes on the card*]
Stephen	There we are. Now I've got it.
Julian	There was your card waiting. When I got in. Welcome home.
Stephen	Look don't make me feel bad for sending you a postcard! because you didn't send me a postcard.

VIII

[STEPHEN *and* PAUL]

Stephen	I wonder if he's taken her to lunch in Holland Park.
Paul	Where in Holland Park?
Stephen	A bar. Sounds like one of his girl friends.
Paul	I know.
Stephen	Have you been there?
Paul	No. What's it like?
Stephen	It's like Bluebeard's castle.
Paul	What?
Stephen	I mean he takes all his serious attempts there. I spent a whole day there once.
Paul	What's it like?
Stephen	It's like a cross between a detoxicated opium den and the copper kettle. Moorish screens. Brass tables. Sofas. Dying palms. A dozing cat. Bits of Church furniture. Ecclesiastical bric-a-brac. Bentwood chairs. Jacobean beams. Mock Persian carpets stapled to the back of pews. Full of boys like him and girls like Nell.
Paul	How do you know he's taken her there?

Stephen	I know. The book matches'll turn up. You see I know what things are going to be like. He didn't ring me. So I rang him at two-thirty.
Paul	In the morning?
Stephen	Yeah. I'm sorry. I'm sorry, he said. I put the phone down. Then later I made a transfer charge call. So he'd think I was in a phone box. I heard him put the phone down. Then I got dressed and went out. It had been raining. I was cold. I went out to make a call from a phone box. So he could hear that sound, that infuriating sound before the money is inserted. And then let him know it was me and then put the phone down. But I didn't believe that the phone box <u>would</u> be out of order as I had imagined. <u>Would</u> be broken, and the next, and the next street. And that I would be walking the streets in the wet until five in the morning and it would be exactly as I had imagined. I went into the casualty department at St. Stephen's. 'I'm confused', I said. 'Could you ring this number?' And they did. 'Are you alright? Would you like to see a doctor?' 'No. I don't exactly know where I am . . . could you just . . . here's my phone book . . . ring this . . . no, <u>not</u> . . . <u>not</u> at that number but at – oh, where is it? Here we are – at <u>this</u> number – he'll be there and ask him to come and get me'. 'Sit down. Have some tea'. 'No, I'm alright. Actually don't make that call. I'm in the driving seat again. I just wanted to know if such help was available. Thank you. Thank you. In case of emergency . . . such as has just occurred'. And then I walked some more and then another broken phone box somewhere behind Olympia. And this young man was walking down the street and he waited for me. What do you do? Do you want a drink? I've just got off the bus. Where are you going? Battersea. You're going the wrong way. He was Scots. I thought I was hallucinating. The revenge was too much. What do you do? Oh . . . You? I write stories and poems. Bleak stories and poems I write. He was thin. And I suppose drunk. I suppose. I couldn't tell. He was soaked through. I didn't want it to happen. What's the matter? I've had a row with someone. Oh, I've just got off a bus. Where are we? Are you all right? Do you know where you are? Aye. We were at home. Do you want a drink? A scotch? It's Irish. Aye. Shall we go to bed? Aye. Do you want this drink? No. And then of course. Suddenly. I don't like this. Where's the light gone? I said, shall I put it out? It went out. I don't like this. Are you all right? Yes of course I'm all right. I don't like this. What's the time it says? Five o'clock. I don't

like this, I'm married. What's the time? Five o'clock. No, it's not. Yes, it is. It's my birthday. I'm twenty-six. I'll have to go. I don't know what this is. Don't worry about this. I'm not. Do you feel bad? Not at all. Not at all. Where am I? Tell me where to go. You're miles away. I've got to go. I so wanted him to go. But I tried to persuade him to stay. His clothes were wet through. I wasn't very convincing. It was a cashmere overcoat. I got this in Brick Lane. Ten pounds it cost. I haven't any money. You'd better stay. I'm depressed. The answer to depression is suicide. Why are you depressed? The row. I've got to go. What's going on? Will I get a bus? It's quarter past five! Give me directions. We kissed. 'A fond kiss'. He came from Glasgow. Why didn't I give him any money? I had money. Why didn't I give it to him? He was thin and poor. Tell me.

Paul   I don't know.

IX

[STEPHEN *and* JULIAN]

Stephen   Hello.

Julian   Can I walk down with you?

Stephen   Yeah. Yeah.

Julian   It's nice to see you.

Stephen   Mmm . . .

Julian   It is. You don't know how nice it is.

Stephen   Don't please. I can't. Please.

Julian   You haven't seen me for four weeks. It's nice to see you.

Stephen   Don't Julian.
                  [JULIAN *is crying*]

Stephen   What's the matter?

Julian   I can't bear it.

Stephen   What?

Julian   She won't see me now. I can't bear it, Stephen. Don't, someone'll see.

Stephen   What does that matter?

Julian   She won't see me.

Stephen	Has she gone back to Dobbin?
Julian	Mm . . . Keith. I think so. We did go to Italy together.
Stephen	Ha! What? Ha!
Julian	You knew.
Stephen	I didn't know.
Julian	You did know.
Stephen	I really didn't know.
Julian	You did know.
Stephen	I really didn't know. I know now, though. It doesn't matter. [*Pause*] That was a dirty bloody trick you know.
Julian	What could I do?
Stephen	Not go.
Julian	How could I not?
Stephen	I bet the first coat you ever wore was reversible.
Julian	Don't. I don't think I can bear it, Stephen.
Stephen	Yes. It must be unbearable. Come on. Come on.
Julian	No.
Stephen	Why do I want this abasement?
Julian	I don't know. You tell me. I don't want it.
Stephen	What?
Julian	What you said.
Stephen	It's the thought of your prostituting intimacies. 'With all my heart'. I can hear you say it. Re-running conversations you've had with me. Do you know what it feels like to know a year of your life is being spunked over someone else on the beach at Lerici?
Julian	Have I done this to punish myself?
Stephen	You mean like a copy-cat murder? I dunno. I should think so . . . I still can't help loving the idea of you. The idea of something real in you. That was recently there in you. That is in you. Come on.

X

[STEPHEN *and* JULIAN]

Stephen	[*Offering* JULIAN *a drink*] Here.
Julian	No.
Stephen	Go on.
Julian	No.
Stephen	Well, why did you come round?
Julian	I don't know. Is it late?
Stephen	Must be.
Julian	How late?
Stephen	Three . . .
Julian	This is just a bundle of misery. Why is she doing it? is she confused? Is she wicked? Fucking me over – like I've fucked you over. You can feel satisfied now.
Stephen	No. I don't feel satified. I'm apprehensive. Yes. Of you. Again. But if you start anything. I warn you. I'll join straight in. You've taken all my sexuality and wasted it in . . . Nell. She's had me through you.
Julian	I can't bear it.
Stephen	Drink this then. Let's go to sleep.
Julian	No. No.
Stephen	You just reject everything I have to offer. The drink. The blanket. I don't do for you. And you have to reject even these comforts. You don't give anything. I only take by giving and you can't even take this. I can't get her for you. I can't go on being punished for this. Ring <u>her</u>. Punish <u>her</u>. Ring bloody Keith. Give <u>him</u> a basinful. Drink this.
Julian	No. I'm going home. Thanks. I'm going to blow myself away. Perhaps that will satisfy everyone.

XI

[NELL *and* JULIAN]

Nell	Angel.
Julian	I came hoping to see Keith, actually. Actually.
Nell	Did you? Why should you want to see Keith?

Julian	Because I did. Alright?
Nell	If you try to see Keith, I'll never see you or speak to you again. Ever. <u>Do you understand</u>?
Julian	Why are you doing this?
Nell	What, doing what?
Julian	Why did you ring me?
Nell	Because I wanted to see you. I missed you.
Julian	Did you?
Nell	I'm sorry. I shouldn't have then.
Julian	No. No. No. Listen, Nell. Listen.
Nell	Yes.
Julian	Listen Nell. If you weren't with Keith, who would you be with?
Nell	Oh dear. Don't be silly. You know.
Julian	I don't know.
Nell	You do.
Julian	Honestly. Really. Really? . . . Please.
Nell	You know I can't.
Julian	But It's over between you and Keith.
Nell	Is it?
Julian	I know it is. It can't be going to go on forever. Not now.
Nell	No. I can't see it lasting forever. But you know . . . I love Keith.
Julian	Stop it. Stop it.
Nell	But you must know that I do.
Julian	I don't want to hear.
Nell	Well don't.
Julian	[*Pause*] And what about me?
Nell	And you. And you.
Julian	Please. I'll do anything. I'll wait.
Nell	Angel.
Julian	I will. I'll wait.

Nell	Would you?
Julian	I will. I've said I will, I'll wait until it's finished. You told me it was finished between you and Keith.
Nell	When did I say that?
Julian	In Italy, virtually . . . I'd just . . .
Nell	What?
Julian	I'd like to . . . again. I'd like to see your face change because of me. I saw it light up because of me. At the door. I just want to have that effect on you again. That's all. I just want to fuck you to see you change. Your eyes hollow and your skin and your mouth. Please, Nell.
Nell	Look, Keith's coming back tomorrow.
Julian	I don't care. Let me stay the night. Please.
Nell	No.
Julian	Then why did you ring? Are you mad or what?
Nell	And if things are different between him and me, it's because of . . . this.
Julian	What?
Nell	Look, you'll have to go.
Julian	No.
Nell	Julian.
Julian	No.
Nell	Julian.
Julian	No.
Nell	Alright. Alright.

XII

[NELL *and* PAUL]

Nell	They call it an abortion. It's an abortion. My mother calls it an infection. A miscarriage is what it is usually known by. But it's a spontaneous abortion. I would have had a termination anyway. I don't want a baby. Anyway, I think probably I've got a slim chance, so they say. I suffer from cervical incompetence. I've got to have it done. I'm bleeding.

Paul	Nell.
Nell	I'm strong you know.
Paul	Are you? Where's Keith?
Nell	He's coming down. He's been very kind. He's coming with me.
Paul	Julian?
Nell	He doesn't know . . . yes I suppose it could be. What about Julian?

XIII

[STEPHEN *and* PAUL]

Stephen	Tell me what to do, he said. Speak to her. I'll write. Don't write, speak. I rang her girlfriend.
Paul	Who?
Stephen	She says she never gave him any reason to hope. I can't understand what's going on in her mind. But I suppose third parties don't count in these matters. He spoke to her. Then rang asking me for a drink. When I arrived. He was . . . they were at the other end of the bar with that look of relief on his face that is his main reason for relating to people at all. I, de trop clearly. I went knowing he'd ring at eleven. He did. I didn't answer. He rang back at twelve-fifteen. I answer. He says can I ring you back in a quarter of an hour? He had to go and see the man. He does dutifully. Ring. Christ. And doesn't want to speak. He's doped out and tired and full of hope. What on earth is she doing? I'm not sophisticated, you know.
Paul	She wants the best of both worlds. Isn't that what we all want?
Stephen	Really.
Paul	Stephen, don't be such a kid. For Nell it's like the two-thirty at Newmarket. It's either Dobbin or Boy Blue. I think she's afraid of being thrown by Boy Blue. I give you 6-to-4 on Dobbin. Always excluding the possibility of a suitable outsider.
Stephen	I think she says things – so he says – like 'if we're fated to be together, we will be. No matter what happens I'll always love you'. Ghastly things like that.
Paul	She's trying to draw it to close.
Stephen	Why?

Paul	Well, she does owe Keith. And she does love him. And it must be faced, Stephen, that Keith must reach those parts of Nell that Julian doesn't get to.
Stephen	They're getting a joint mortgage. Nell and Keith.
Paul	No, they're not. A joint mortgage is the fashionable way of saying I do.

XIV

[PAUL *and* JULIAN]
[PAUL *reading a letter*]

Paul	'Angel, the time has come . . . ' I don't want to read this.
Julian	Go on. Please. I don't know what to do, Paul. When I opened it and read 'the time has come' I thought.
Paul	I could see you might. I really don't want to read it Julian.
Julian	I've told her I'll wait. Is she a bitch? Is she? Look Paul, you know her. Tell me. Read it.
Paul	'I've never hurt so much . . . ! No-one has made me hurt so much!' Does she accept all the blame?
Julian	Yes.
Paul	[*Laughs*] Yes. 'I'm sorry. My fault. No blame'. she certainly has a flowing pen . . . Ah . . .
Julian	What?
Paul	'I only hope I have the strength of will not to see you again'. [*Reads more*] Did you know she'd been in hospital before this?
Julian	Yes. But not . . . it was mine. I know it.
Paul	How do you know?
Julian	Paul. You know. Because one knows.
Paul	Does one?
Julian	Yes.
Paul	Have you shown this to anyone else? Have you shown this to Stephen?
Julian	Yes.
Paul	You've shown this to Stephen! Did he know about . . . before this?

Julian	Yes. What am I going to do, Paul?
Paul	What's the point of saying things like if you don't watch out you're going to get into trouble one day. Nell, I know about. There's nothing to be said for Nell. Nell's what used to be called a free spirit. She's like Gwendolyn Harleth as seen by Rebecca West in a book which Virago found too dull to republish, 'Was she beautiful, or not beautiful'. It's Nell spelt with a K.
Julian	What do you know about Nell?
Paul	You know there isn't any ownership involved. I know a lot about Nell. I even like Nell. I can still say I like her. I do. I have, and I do, and Stephen doesn't know and we have since you met and we have since you got back from Italy. But that's between me and Nell. Why didn't you keep this between you and Nell. What's Stephen done to <u>you</u>? He <u>isn't</u> your father, you know. You're going to get yourself into trouble. You are sometime. It's no good saying anything to Nell. She's degenerate as far as personal feelings go.

XV

[JULIAN]

Julian	I'm in purgatory. It lifts momentarily, and then I wonder. Why doesn't she ring? Then I think about Stephen . . . I know it was mine. I know. Dad. I hate Stephen. I'll ring him, he'll understand. Why doesn't he leave me alone? How could she do it? I'm going to ring her. I rang her. Ansaphone, ansaphone. She encompasses me. Why? She loves me. Why? Stephen. Why? Stephen. I rang him. I've got to go to bed I say. Why? He rings back. I can't take him. I don't say anything. Why has she done this? I hate her. Dad. I hate him so much. I asked Stephen should I buy her flowers. I'm wrecked. Oh please where is she? She's <u>fucked</u> me. And I'm in trouble with Stephen. Stephen. Why doesn't he leave me alone? I need to talk to him. He pisses me off. I'm not ringing dad. I do hate him. Stephen's so fucking selfish. The rubbish he talks. I'm not seeing him. Fuck him. If he's angry, good. I'm fucking angry. Really fucking angry. Where is she? Why has she done this? Shall I ring her? I really hate her. Fuck them. I'm in torment. Where is she? I'm not ringing Stephen. What'll he do? Fuck him. Dad. I've put a message on her machine. I can't cope, I can't live without her. I hate her. I hate Stephen. Dad. I really <u>do hate.</u>

XVI

[STEPHEN *and* JULIAN]

Stephen	No.
Julian	What?
Stephen	She isn't better. She isn't more beautiful. She isn't cleverer. She isn't – than you. You're fighting her for possession of yourself.
Julian	Yeah? I saw two people in the street just now kissing, flirting, laughing. An ugly young man and a young woman looking much older than their age. She without teeth – he with bad teeth. Unkempt, dirty, drunk. Like children. Oblivious to everyone else. Why them? I've got nobody. Look, everyone is married. I'm losing her and you. Why do people tell you things and then not help you? I know she wants me really. I know.
Stephen	Oh my dear, shall we never be able to . . . Shall you always be the thing you're . . . Shall you not want me? Shall we always be. Oh my dear, what a God awful pity, eh? That people suited and yet not suited. In rebellion. Struggling. You're like one's child. I can't desert you. This amidst all the welter of hate, envy, nerves, frustration. People will say you're very silly and spoilt – but they won't have seen the glimpses, will they? They won't. They'll perceive the charm. The looks. But they won't have seen you look ugly or have seen you when you've squeezed a few tears out. Or how bright you are or how painful your self-knowledge is. We colluded in a fantasy. We are colluding in a fantasy.
Julian	She wants me. I know she does really. But she's too scared to leave him.
Stephen	I'm like a dog scratching at the door.
Julian	She is. She's . . .
Stephen	I know she hasn't finished with you yet. I'm not certain you can honestly say you're finished with her. What if she arrives with her suitcases?
Julian	I'd be glad of the opportunity to shut the door.
Stephen	You wouldn't.
Julian	What do you know what I'll do? Why do you think you know everything about me? What do you want?

Stephen   Ownership of you is what I want, alright? OK? Does that suit
you? You want to say it too – say it to someone as mediocre
as you are. Someone you think of as <u>really</u> mediocre, really.
'Is she better than me?' – You don't mean it. You think she's
mediocre which I don't think of you really, you fucking,
fucking bastard. I don't think you even think that about her.
Nell. Do you? Yours is not as unhinged an obsession, is it? It's
much more acceptable. But you still want to say it – so's you
can say I've suffered too. I've been fucked over, she's fucked
me over. You're storing up things she's never imagined,
aren't you? To say to her eventually. But you want her to fuck
you over so you can say 'I've paid. I deserve worse in most
instances, but in this one I've paid for the others'. And when
and if she says it's over <u>again</u>, I'll be there. You've got right on
your side, haven't you, really? With all your pretence and
free thinking, you're right, you're right. The legacy of
Romanticism . . . What Lady Caroline Lamb said about Byron
has lent glamour to all the cheap irresponsibilities of people
like you and Nell ever since, without acknowledgement that
Byron actually produced something at least as substantial as
all the misery he must have caused. But you're so right. So
right. But even mad, red, rich, dead, not very cred Shelley
wasn't right on about everything. The avoidances in 'The
Symposium' – what about them? Atheism, freedom, feminism,
free love – up to a point. But there was something left to
answer and there was no one living whose ideas he could
colonise in <u>that</u> respect. What about the boy at Syon House?
The Master at Eton? Although, even after having written the
coldest hearted poem any man could have written to his
wife, he at least saved her from dying from a miscarriage.
Something you would be too doped out or preoccupied to
cope with. What about Hogg and Trewlawney and Williams?
I think it was a drowning of convenience. I think there
was something irreconcilable. You know there's nothing
intrinsically special about you. You haven't earned this
attitude by anything you've done – except swim the mile.
Your attitude is a result of money spent on your quite
inadequate education and your inability to jump class with
any grace. In spite of the dope and the street credibility,
your mind is essentially suburban. Nuclear fall-out. I love
it. It's the only classless thing there is. Do you know I don't
know whether or not anything of what I've been saying
has any basis in truth at all. They were true words when I
spoke them. Or the feelings underpinning them were true.

There was feeling. But what I was saying. The opinions, the rationalisations, I think they were just ways of trying to say something else really. I don't think what I'm saying now is . . . I think it's genuine enough information. But lies. I think. Not deliberate – don't have the words – or am forbidden them. How can one just keep saying I love you or I need you or I love you. Over and over. You'd be bored. One has to say other things when one wants not to speak at all but to say please or help or come or love or please or cry. Over and over and over.

Julian   Stephen. Do you remember once inviting me to tell you to fuck off. Fuck off. Just fuck off.
[STEPHEN *picks up the knife that he used to open a letter in the first scene*]

Julian   Christ. Stephen. Stephen.

Stephen   Don't move. Paul! Paul! Don't move.
[PAUL *enters*]

Paul   Stephen.

Stephen   He's OK, it's OK. Don't you move. It's OK. Now see this. If I wanted to I could scar you in the only way that would matter to you. Look at me. I'm your mirror for the moment. Look at yourself. I could. It's alright. I'm not going to. Here, Paul.
[*Gives the knife to* PAUL]
Paul.

Paul   Stephen.

Stephen   He can't be loved. He won't be loved. Will you? You see, he won't be loved. You won't.

Paul   Stephen.

Stephen   No. [*To* JULIAN.] Listen.
Little Boy Blue come blow up your horn
The sheep in the meadow, the cows in the corn
But where's the boy who looks after the sheep?
He's under the haystack fast asleep.
[*Pause*]
Will I wake him? No, not I
For if I do he is sure to cry.

Isn't that great?

In the Blue

Characters

Stewart
Michael

Suggestion of a room. On the floor, books, clothes, magazines, a towel, newspapers, records, tapes, a tray, postcards, cups etc. Not too slovenly. No furniture.

I

Stewart	Right then.
Michael	Are you going to ring?
Stewart	I said I'd ring.
Michael	But are you going to?
Stewart	Yeah. Of course I am, what's the matter with you?
Michael	I'd better give you the right number then.
Stewart	I've got it.
Michael	No you haven't. Here.
Stewart	Well fuck me.
Michael	Yeah.
Stewart	What you do that for? What a liberty. What you do that for? Fuck me.
Michael	Haven't you ever done that?
Stewart	No I haven't got a phone. Anyway I wouldn't. Why did you do that?
Michael	I don't know. In case you rang. I don't know.
Stewart	But you asked me to ring.
Michael	I know. Will you ring?
Stewart	I dunno now.
Michael	I thought you wouldn't.
Stewart	I said I fucking would. Where's the number?
Michael	Where's my pen. I can't find my pen. You got a pen? Thanks.
Stewart	Honest. You. Honest.
Michael	There we are. Thanks.
Stewart	Right then.
Michael	You off?

Stewart	Yes.
Michael	Are you going to ring?
Stewart	I said I would.
Michael	Or . . .
Stewart	D'you want to leave it then?
Michael	If you want to.
Stewart	Do you want to? Give me your number.
Michael	Or perhaps.
Stewart	Well . . . I'm off . . . I'll phone you . . . Shall I?
Michael	Sorry? What? Oh, yes. You've got the number have you?
Stewart	Yes. Oh no. Where is it? What did I do with it? [MICHAEL *picks a scrap of paper from the floor and gives it to* STEWART] Oh yeah. Thanks. I'll see you then.
Michael	Yes.
Stewart	Thank you for the . . .
Michael	Oh that's . . . Listen ring first OK? Don't . . .
Stewart	No.
Michael	It might be . . .
Stewart	Yeah.
Michael	You probably won't ring anyway.
Stewart	What do you say that for? You never know. Do you? Eh? Anyway thanks. OK?
Michael	Yes.
Stewart	And I'm sorry about the . . .
Michael	Oh that's . . . Listen take care.
Stephen	Of what?
Michael	I wonder if he'll ring. He might ring. He won't ring. Why should he ring? What if he rings?
Stewart	Have you given me the wrong number?
Michael	No.

Stewart	Only I noticed the number when I came in. You gonna muck me about?
Michael	Or . . . Do you want the number?
Stewart	No.
Michael	Or . . . Do you want the number?
Stewart	No. Thanks.
Michael	Or . . .
Stewart	Here we are. OK?
Michael	What's your name?
Stewart	Stewart.
Michael	You don't look like a Stewart. Do you charge?
Stewart	What?
Michael	You should charge. You've got the kind of flat and the kind of records. And you live in the kind of street.
Stewart	What?
Michael	It's so beautiful this street.
Stewart	What are you called?
Michael	Stewart.
Stewart	No. Come on. Come on.
Michael	No. It's so beautiful this street in this weather.
Stewart	Is it? If you think so.
Michael	I do. What are they, the trees?
Stewart	Trees. Street trees. Are you a student?
Michael	I wonder they haven't sold these off. These flats. These cold water flats.
Stewart	Why?
Michael	They generally do. Sell them.
Stewart	Oh yeah.
Michael	They do. Do them up. Sell them. They do.
Stewart	What do you mean cold water flats? This isn't a cold water flat.
Michael	That's what they are.

Stewart	You're not in New York you know. What <u>do</u> you do then?
Michael	I like these flats up all those stone stairs. Do you have neighbours?
Stewart	Why won't you tell me?
Michael	I like the door knob, the broken glass.
Stewart	Eh?
Michael	This is just the kind of flat where the guy's on the game.
Stewart	Do you want to pay?
Michael	Yeah ... Or ...
Stewart	I might see you then.
Michael	Or ...
Stewart	Thanks.
Michael	Or ...
Stewart	No. I'm not.
Michael	Or ...
Stewart	Look at all these books.
Michael	Or ...
Stewart	I'm off then.
Michael	Or ...
Stewart	You read all these then do you?
Michael	Or ...
Stewart	Do you want to leave it then?
Michael	Or ...
Stewart	D'you wanna leave it then?
Michael	Or ...
Stewart	Do you wanna leave it then?
Michael	I don't know, do you?
Stewart	I don't mind, do you?
Michael	I don't know, do you?
Stewart	I don't mind, do you?
Michael	I don't know. Or ...

Stewart	Shall I see you then?
Michael	Perhaps.
Stewart	See you then.
Michael	Or . . .
Stewart	I can see when you're excited.
Michael	Or . . .
Stewart	I've got plans for you.
Michael	Or . . .
Stewart	What are you in to?
Michael	I'm in to you at the moment. What are you in to?
Stewart	Yeah.
Michael	Or . . .
Stewart	No I'm not.
Michael	Or . . .
Stewart	Are you scared? What are you scared of?
Michael	Or it could be . . .
Stewart	Ssh . . . ssh.
Michael	What?
Stewart	You'll wake him up.
Michael	Who?
Stewart	Lenny.
Michael	Christ! Who's he?
Stewart	The fella I share with.
Michael	What?
Stewart	Ssh, come on. He won't wake up. He won't mind if he does. He'll be quite happy.
Michael	No.
Stewart	Yeah! Come on.
Michael	Or . . .
Stewart	Right then!
Michael	Oh yes!

Stewart	I'm off then . . . [*Pause*] OK . . . [*Pause*] OK . . .
Michael	What? Oh yes. Yes.
	Or . . .
Stewart	Do you want me to ring?
Michael	Or . . . Why don't you ring?
Stewart	No. I won't bother.
Michael	Or . . .
Stewart	Do you want to come in?
Michael	Or . . .
Stewart	Are we here then?
Michael	Or . . .
Stewart	This is it, then.
Michael	Or . . .
Stewart	Do you live by yourself?
Michael	Or . . .
Stewart	Mind the stairs.
Michael	Or . . .
Stewart	Is this all yours then?
Michael	Or . . .
Stewart	I don't want to hurt you.
Michael	Or . . .
	[*Slight pause*]
Stewart	Are you a student?

II

Michael	I didn't think you'd ring.
Stewart	I said I'd ring you.
Michael	I know you did. I still didn't think you would . . . Why should you? I wouldn't have.

Stewart	Well there's the difference between us, isn't it? I wouldn't have said I would ring if I wasn't going to ring.
Michael	You didn't say much on the phone.
Stewart	Wasn't much to say.
Michael	You came round quick enough.
Stewart	I didn't.
Michael	Oh.
Stewart	I took my time. Anyway, what's it matter? I wanted to come round.
Michael	Good then, you're here.
Stewart	Yeah that's right. Well then.
Michael	What?
Stewart	Come here.
Michael	No.
Stewart	No, suit yourself. I can take my time. You still got all these books then.
Michael	Yeah.
Stewart	The Gift Relationship. From human blood to social policy. When was that written? When the world was young? What have you been doing with yourself?
Michael	Do you mean today?
Stewart	Today, yesterday. What's the matter with you? Do you want me to go? I'm not going.
Michael	Or . . . it could be . . .
Stewart	I'm gasping for a fag. D'you smoke?
Michael	I don't. I'm sorry. I know. Let's go and get some. Why don't you go and get some?
Stewart	I'm skint.
Michael	I've got money.
Stewart	Let's go for a drink then.
Michael	Oh.
Stewart	Yeah! C'mon.
Michael	Okay.

Stewart	D'you play pool? I'll teach you to play pool.
Michael	I can play pool.
Stewart	You can't play pool. Can you play pool?
Michael	Of course. Can you?
Stewart	Of course. I'm brilliant. I've kept myself in fags playing pool.
Michael	Or it could be . . . What is it?
Stewart	I think I've got something in my eye.
Michael	Come here.
Stewart	No.
Michael	Pull your lid over it.
Stewart	No
Michael	Go on. Now how is it?
Stewart	I think it's better. Thanks. No it's still there.
Michael	Come here. Come here.
Stewart	No.
Michael	Come on. Hold still. There we are, look. There we are. OK?
Stewart	Thanks.
Michael	Or . . . Can you whistle?
Stewart	Course I can whistle.
Michael	You know, like this. Can you whistle like this? [*Demonstrates*]
Stewart	Of course I can.
Michael	Go on then. [*Attempts and fails*]
Michael	I thought you couldn't.
Stewart	What does that mean?
Michael	Or . . .
Stewart	How are you?
Michael	Good, very good.
Stewart	Good.

Michael	I wish you hadn't asked that.
Stewart	Why?
Michael	Now I don't feel so good. I felt fine, now I feel fairly fucking terrible. Or . . . What if he keeps his cigarettes in his teeshirt? Oh my God. Or . . .
Stewart	I came down two years ago.
Michael	Or . . . More brutal exchanges don't you think? Regardless of my views on the matter. Or . . .
Stewart	I'm not living anywhere special.
Michael	Or . . . Sometimes I think I'm as intelligent as I pretend to be. Or . . .
Stewart	I came down with this young lassie. We travelled down together. After I got picked up by the police, she went back. I was bevvying a bit. No money. No kip. You couldn't blame her. I was sent down. I expect she's alright.
Michael	Or . . .
Stewart	I was in this doss in London and one morning I went to take a piss, and someone came in and said where's Lenny and tried to kick the cubicle door in. So I went into the next cubicle and I pulled myself up to look about, and there he was, Lenny, sitting with his head rolled back and a needle beside him on the floor. Then the superintendent rang the police and said he's dead as far as I can see. Take your time anyway. He's no use to anyone. An old man died in the same doss, so the authorities came to take the body away. They handed him as far as the landing and one of them says 'hey up' to the men below and tipped him over the bannister. They never caught him. They put him in a box and carted him off.
Michael	Or . . .
Stewart	I like being with you. I do. D'you hear me? You. What about you. Hey.
Michael	You're beautiful. I know that. Or . . . I thought of having my ears pierced.
Stewart	That's a bit strong isn't it?
Michael	I should have thought it was a bit passé.

Stewart	What?
Michael	Old fashioned.
Stewart	It is.
Michael	Then why did you have yours pierced?
Stewart	It wasn't passé when I had it done.
Michael	Who did it?
Stewart	Lenny.
Michael	How?
Stephen	Stuck a needle through it. I'll do yours for you.
Michael	No you won't. I'll get the charge nurse to do it with a suture needle. Or it could be . . .
Stewart	What's that?
Michael	A postcard from a friend of mine. He says we haven't seen each other for a year. And he says he's moving.
Stewart	Where's he moving to?
Michael	Tottenham.
Stewart	That's nice. You'll be able to go for a holiday.
Michael	He says the postcard looks like me.
Stewart	Let's have a see. Who is it?
Michael	Keats. It's not my fault we haven't seen each other for a year.
Stewart	Who is he?
Michael	We were in college together. We haven't seen each other for a year: must be a year since he got married. We were all in college together. I was the best man. I bought a suit. Humiliating eh? It was like a footballer's wedding. Looked like a beer advert. Perhaps I should get married. Bastard.
Stewart	Oh, I see.
Michael	What?
Stewart	Nothing, nothing.
Michael	Or . . . Can't you get a job?

Stewart	I don't want a job. I've had a job.
Michael	I'm sorry. I'm sorry.
Stewart	That's OK.
Michael	I just meant. Well.
Stewart	What?
Michael	You seem.
Stewart	What?
Michael	I don't know. You're . . . Oh . . . Money . . . You're so . . . I want. Oh . . . Are you OK?
Stewart	I'm OK. The giro'll do for me. I've had jobs.
Michael	Or . . . What is it?
Stewart	Nothing.
Michael	You can tell me.
Stewart	Nothing. I'm alright.
Michael	Or . . . You're a lazy fucker.
Stewart	Well you'd know.
Michael	You take the action for the deed, that's your trouble. Or . . .
Stewart	Look, Lenny was already on it. I don't do smack or anything much. I can take it or leave it. I'd rather have a drink which is just as well on my income. What business is it of yours anyway?
Michael	Or . . .
Stewart	Look?
Michael	What?
Stewart	Sweating.
Michael	That's alright.
Stewart	No it isn't. I don't like it.
Michael	Come here. [*Takes his hand and licks it*]

Stewart	You . . . [*Makes a fist at him, joking*]
Michael	Or it could be . . . then it could be . . . Or it could be.
Stewart	Do you want me to stay?
Michael	Or it could be . . . No. Or . . . No.
Stewart	What's the matter?
Michael	Or . . .
Stewart	What is it?
Michael	Or . . . No. Or . . .
Stewart	It's alright.
Michael	No.
Stewart	Come on. Come on. What's the matter?
Michael	No.
Stewart	Come on.
Michael	No.
Stewart	What is it? What is it?
Michael	How am I going to get through? A lot of people spend their lives just in drink . . . Don't have any afterwards. When you drop dead. Do you want everlasting life? Just got to grow old when you come to think of it. Does that worry you? I think the problems start when you start listening to yourself. I know who I am but I don't know where I am. I'm all over the fucking place. This is awful. I could . . . Go away. I have to be by myself. If I could put myself in touch with my feelings I'd probably kill you. It's when you're not here I want you. I want to reach across and hold on to you. To hold you. Only I seem not to be allowed any feelings. I seem not to have feelings except sentimental ones. Or I seem only to have feelings. I seem to be all feelings. Don't please. I'm frightened, I'm OK. I walk around and even now when I'm talking . . . If someone had died I'd have some reason for this. I'd have some right to this feeling. If you died. If someone had just died even. If you were dead. But I haven't first call. You see . . . I think . . . You see to dwell upon the ulterior motive for the sake of truth is . . . To overemphasize that everything is dependent upon motive. To emphasize <u>that</u> truth is to deny that ulterior

motive does not only produce results for the self. To think altruism is only worth measuring by ulterior motive is wrong. Stupid. Or to deny spontaneity. I'll have to get it together. How am I going to get it together?

Stewart You will.

Michael Do you think so?

Stewart You will.

Michael Never mind. I'm in pieces. Not even pieces, scraps. I'll have to get it together. How am I going to get it together?

Stewart You will.

Michael Do you think so? I don't think I ever will.

Stewart You will.

Michael Yet there's another part of me that doesn't give a fuck.

III

Stewart I've been for a drink.

Michael Good.

Stewart I've got to have a piss.

Michael Good.

Stewart I feel sick.

Michael Great.

Stewart Michael.

Michael What?

Stewart Michael.
[MICHAEL *goes to him*]

Michael Sit down, come on.

Stewart No it's alright, I'm alright thanks.

Michael You alright?

Stewart Yeah, you're a pal. I'm going for a piss OK. What's the matter?

Michael Now I feel sick.

Stewart	No, don't feel sick.
Michael	I think I'm going to be sick.
Stewart	No you're not.
Michael	How do you know I'm not going to be sick?
Stewart	Are you gonna be sick? Michael. Don't be sick. I'm not going to be sick. I'm never sick. Are you alright Michael? Oh, Michael, I'm going for a piss. You coming for a piss? I feel rotten. Ah'm gonna put my fingers down my throat.
Michael	Now I feel really sick. Or . . . What is it?
Stewart	Leave it will you.
Michael	Hang on. Hang on. Hang on!
Stewart	Just leave it.
Michael	What's the matter?
Stewart	You are.
Michael	Or . . .
Stewart	I'm going for a drink.
Michael	Oh yes.
Stewart	Yes.
Michael	Oh Christ!
Stewart	Yes.
Michael	Look, why don't you go for a drink?
Stewart	I am going for a drink.
Michael	Well go for a fucking drink then. Or . . . are we going to the pictures then?
Stewart	I don't know.
Michael	Well do you want to go to the pictures?
Stewart	I don't know, why should I have to make all the fucking decisions?
Michael	Well why should I have to?
Stewart	Well why should I?

Michael	Don't shout.
Stewart	I'll shout. [*Pause*]
Michael	What is it?
Stewart	I'm fucking confused I can tell you. I've never felt like this before, I can tell you. About any fucker. [*Cries*]
Michael	Why? [*Softly*] Why? [*Goes to him*]
Stewart	Get off. [*Struggling*] You're so fucking clever you are, you ought to be done away with you. You're sick. D'you know that? You're sick. You're sick, d'you know that? You're sick. You are. You're really sick. You're sick. You really are.
Michael	Don't.
Stewart	Do you love me? You love every fucker you do.
Michael	Come on. Come on, let's go to the pictures. Come on. Or . . .
Stewart	I have to thank you. No. I do. No don't fuck about. Thanks. Thanks. Hold still. Thanks.
Michael	Or . . . Hello.
Stewart	Don't start anything.
Michael	Nice to see you.
Stewart	Don't Michael. Alright?
Michael	Very nice.
Stephen	I've put the kettle on.
Michael	I've been everywhere looking for you. I've been to the pub. I've been to the Irish pub. I've been to all the snooker halls round here. I've been to Sid's Snooker Saloon. You looking for Stewart? You've just missed him. I've been down Portobello to see if you were scoring. I've been in the Elgin, I've been down All Saints Road. I went over to Coldharbour Lane. All up the Railton Road. I came back here again. I nearly rang the law. I've had a really good time. You?
Stewart	What you go over there for? I haven't been over there. How long is it since I've been over there?
Michael	I don't know. Where have you been?

Stewart	Look I was on the piss. I didn't think I'd better come back.
Michael	Where'd you end up?
Stewart	I don't know.
Michael	You know.
Stewart	I don't. Look it's none of your business where I've been, where I ended up.
Michael	Just tell me.
Stewart	I'm not telling you, Michael. And if you were so concerned, you should have shown some concern earlier. I can go out by my own if I want to, OK? Anyway, I asked you to come with me. I wanted you to come. I'm not staying here with you pulling me to pieces one minute and not talking to me the next. You talk about commitment. You haven't spoken to me for three days. What am I to do?
Michael	Why didn't you ring up?
Stewart	Because I didn't want to.
Michael	I'll pull it on. I will one of these days.
Stewart	Well you wanted me to go out. Didn't you eh? Didn't you?
Michael	I didn't.
Stewart	Didn't you?
Michael	I didn't.
Stewart	Oh yeah? Well why wouldn't you talk to me?
Michael	Where were you, tell me? Please.
Stewart	And anyway, what about you eh? What about you.
Michael	What?
Stewart	You know.
Michael	I don't know. What? There was an old man dying, I worked on.
Stewart	You didn't tell me.
Michael	Did you mind then?
Stewart	No, of course I don't mind. But you didn't tell me.
Michael	You haven't said anything about it since.
Stewart	Well I'm saying it now. I had to ring to find out where you were.

Michael	You didn't tell me.
Stewart	To find out if you were working on. I had to make a right fool of myself.
Michael	How was that making a fool of yourself?
Stewart	Well it was.
Michael	Well, what do you think I was fucking doing last night? And I haven't been to sleep. And I've got to be up all tonight.
Stewart	Now you know what it's like.
Michael	Stewart, I worked all night because an old man was dying and they were shorthanded and I spent most of the day with him and I worked on.
Stewart	You're stupid, you are, anyway.
Michael	What do you mean?
Stewart	You're more qualified than what any of that poxy lot are. What's the matter with you! You've had an education. You give up a top job in the civil service and now you're a hospital fucking orderly.
Michael	Auxilliary.
Stewart	And how long's it gonna last?
Michael	What?
Stewart	What are you going to do next?
Michael	What are you going on about? What am I going to do next? What about you? What are you doing? What do you do all day? Sleep, boozer, betting shop, smoke dope, sleep.
Stewart	But Michael, you haven't got the necessary to be a tosser like me. What are you doing?
Michael	Leave me alone.
Stewart	But you're making a mess of yourself.
Michael	I'm tired.
Stewart	Why'd you give your first job up eh?
Michael	I don't know.
Stewart	Why? Tell me.
Michael	Don't. Please. Really.

Stewart	Go on.
Michael	I think I thought it was wrong. And you know . . . Growth. [*Laughing*] I wanted to do something connected with people. [*Pause*] Where were you?
Stewart	No.
Michael	You've got to tell me.
Stewart	I haven't.
Michael	Tell me.
Stewart	No.
Michael	Alright. Put the kettle on.
Stewart	It's on.
Michael	Go on.
Stewart	It's on, it's on. Do you want me to sing to you? [*Laughter*]
Michael	Where were you?
Stewart	You'll never find out.
Michael	I will.
Stewart	I doubt it. Got a paper?
Michael	There.
Stewart	Oh Christ, I've got to change. Have you got any clean underpants?
Michael	I've stopped wearing them. They're bad for you.
Stewart	Oh aye.
Michael	Am I making the tea?
Stewart	I don't know. Are you?
Michael	Are you?
Stewart	I will if you like.
Michael	I'll do it. Where were you? Tell me.
Stewart	Michael. No.
Michael	Or . . .
Stewart	I'm going.

Michael	Why?
Stewart	Ask yourself.
Michael	Where will you go?
Stewart	Don't worry about me.
Michael	Or . . .
Stewart	I don't know what I'm doing here.
Michael	Don't you?
Stewart	Cut it out Michael will you.
Michael	Well what did you say that for?
Stewart	Because I don't.
Michael	Why don't you?
Stewart	I don't know.
Michael	Why?
Stewart	Stop it, Michael, will you?
Michael	I don't think this is perhaps what we had in mind.
Stewart	I didn't have anything in mind. I think it was you who had things in mind.
Michael	Or . . .
Stewart	I'm going.
Michael	Don't do that.
Stewart	No I'm going.
Michael	Where will you go?
Stewart	Don't worry about me.
Michael	I won't. Or . . .
Stewart	This is stupid this is.
Michael	What is?
Stewart	This is.
Michael	Not as stupid as you. I can't do this. This is hopeless. You're so stupid.
Stewart	Hey you.

Michael	What? What? I'm not scared of you.
Stewart	Not yet you're not.
Michael	What?
Stewart	Alright. Alright.
Michael	Or . . . I thought you were going.
Stewart	I am going.
Michael	I'm glad to hear it.
Stewart	I am.
Michael	Well go on then, fuck off then.
Stewart	I will.
Michael	I wish you would.
Stewart	I will.
Michael	Well go on! Go on! Why don't you just go! Or . . .
Stewart	Right then! If that's the way you see it, you cunt, you're more of a soft prick than I took you for. Oh blimey, Charlie, shall I come over there?
Michael	Oh Christ no!
Stewart	I want to.
Michael	Well I don't. This is like . . . I don't know what this is like. I wish I had the knack of taking opportunities. I can make opportunities. I'm great at making opportunities. Like . . . this is.
Stewart	Don't, Michael.
Michael	I'm alright. Don't come over. Or . . .
Stewart	I'm moving out.
Michael	Don't do that.
Stewart	No. I'm going.
Michael	Where will you go?
Stewart	Don't worry about me.
Michael	Why do you want to do that?

Stewart	Why do you think?
Michael	Or ...
Stewart	See, I can't handle it. I don't know what I'm up to.
Michael	I see.
Stewart	Can't you see what I mean?
Michael	No.
Stewart	Well I'm not up to it. That's for sure.
Michael	Or ... What are you going to do about it?
Stewart	What! About what?
Michael	About me.
Stewart	What about you?
Michael	And you.
Stewart	What about me?
Michael	And me.
Stewart	Cut it out, Michael, will you.
Michael	I suppose one person can't be held responsible for the effect he has on another, wouldn't you say?
Stewart	No, I wouldn't say. I bloody wouldn't say.
Michael	Or ...
Stewart	I'll be off then. OK? Is it OK?
Michael	What are you asking me for?
Stewart	Well come with me.
Michael	Or ...
Stewart	Be nice Michael. Be nice.
Michael	Or ...
Stewart	Why do you want me to go?
Michael	I don't.
Stewart	But you do Michael, I'll go if you'll say.
Michael	I don't.

Stewart	You do.
Michael	I don't! I don't! I don't!
Stewart	You see.
Michael	Or . . . Please.
Stewart	No, for Christ's sake.
Michael	I'll try.
Stewart	No.
Michael	I will.
Stewart	You try.
Michael	It's worse for me.
Stewart	Oh yeah.
Michael	I didn't mean it like that.
Stewart	Oh.
Michael	Don't go.
Stewart	I've got to.
Michael	It is possible.
Stewart	I know.
Michael	It basically seems to depend on whether you can do the washing-up. I'll do the washing-up.
Stewart	Oh blimey. I haven't got it Michael.
Michael	Or . . .
Stewart	Let's sort it out shall we?
Michael	Or . . . Or . . .
Stewart	What do you want to do then?
Michael	Or . . .
Stewart	Am I staying?
Michael	Or . . .
Stewart	Come on let's go.
Michael	Or . . .

Stewart	We'll be alright.
Michael	Or . . .
Stewart	What do you want?
Michael	Or . . .
Stewart	Just tell me!
Michael	Or . . .
Stewart	Why didn't you ring.
Michael	Couldn't.
Stewart	Who brought the letter?
Michael	Me.
Stewart	You?
Michael	I didn't think you'd come.
Stewart	Why didn't you think I'd come?
Michael	You're pretty diffident. Hence the note.
Stewart	You should have rung me. Idiot. [*Laughs*] Fool.
Michael	You didn't ring me. But I'm grateful all the same. Thanks. Honest. Thanks for coming, thanks. Thanks.
Stewart	How have you been?
Michael	Fairly fucking dreadful.
Stewart	Not so bad then.
Michael	You?
Stewart	Oh me. Of course. You know me.
Michael	Don't you want to know?
Stewart	What?
Michael	Why the letter . . .
Stewart	If you like.
Michael	Listen, this is important.
Stewart	I know, Michael. Honest, why do you think I've come over, eh?. Oh Jesus, listen. There's more at stake for me, you know.
Michael	Oh aye.

Stewart	Because you'll eventually get fed up with all this. Bound to. And where will that leave me, eh? Can you answer me that? You alright?
Michael	I'm alright. You alright? [*Laughter*]
Stewart	I brought this back. [*Gives him a book*]
Michael	Did you like it?
Stewart	Quite.
Michael	I can't see why you couldn't have come round. What a bastard thing to do. Why don't you come round? I just can't bear the feeling that you're not coming round. That I'm not going to see you. But what would happen if you did come round? And yet there have been times in the last week when I have so wanted you to be here. Sitting here. When I've thought of things to say to you. Nothing much. Why? Why? But I'm no better than you that's the truth of it. You'd better go hadn't you?
Stewart	I suppose.
Michael	Hadn't you?
Stewart	If you want me to.
Michael	Will you be alright?
Stewart	I'll be fine. I'll ring you.
Michael	Will you.
Stewart	I will. Honest.
Michael	But, will you?
Stewart	I said I would.
Michael	You got the number. Where's the number? You got the number.
Stewart	I've got the number.
Michael	Where's the number. Oh Jesus.
Stewart	Shall I ring you?
Michael	If you want.

Stewart	Do you want me to?
Michael	If you like.
Stewart	You've still got all these books then?
Michael	Do you want to come in?
Stewart	Shall we go then?
Michael	What's your name?
Stewart	Do you want a drink?
Michael	Not very far.
Stewart	By yourself?
Michael	Not very often.
Stewart	Where do you live?
Michael	No. I don't.
Stewart	Where's your jacket?
Michael	I don't want to hurt you. [*Slight pause*]
Stewart	Are you a student?
Michael	Or . . .
Stewart	Michael, Michael, it's hurting, it's hurting.
Michael	It's alright.
Stewart	Michael.
Michael	It's alright.
Stewart	Michael.
Michael	It's alright. Or . . .
Stewart	Come on.
Michael	No.
Stewart	Yes. Come on. Come on. Come on!
Michael	No.
Stewart	Come on, fight. [*Pause*] It's alright. It's alright. [*Pause*] Do you want to leave it then?